Currents

33 1/3 Global

33 1/3 Global, a series related to but independent from **33 1/3**, takes the format of the original series of short, music-based books and brings the focus to music throughout the world. With initial volumes focusing on Japanese and Brazilian music, the series will also include volumes on the popular music of Australia/Oceania, Europe, Africa, the Middle East, and more.

33 1/3 Japan

Series Editor: Noriko Manabe

Spanning a range of artists and genres – from the 1970s rock of Happy End to technopop band Yellow Magic Orchestra, the Shibuya-kei of Cornelius, classic anime series *Cowboy Bebop*, J-Pop/EDM hybrid Perfume, and vocaloid star Hatsune Miku – 33 1/3 Japan is a series devoted to in-depth examination of Japanese popular music of the twentieth and twenty-first centuries.

Published Titles:
Supercell's *Supercell* by Keisuke Yamada
AKB48 by Patrick W. Galbraith and Jason G. Karlin
Yoko Kanno's *Cowboy Bebop Soundtrack* by Rose Bridges
Perfume's *Game* by Patrick St. Michel
Cornelius's *Fantasma* by Martin Roberts
Joe Hisaishi's *My Neighbor Totoro: Soundtrack* by Kunio Hara
Shonen Knife's *Happy Hour* by Brooke McCorkle
Nenes' *Koza Dabasa* by Henry Johnson
Yuming's *The 14th Moon* by Lasse Lehtonen
Toshiko Akiyoshi-Lew Tabackin Big Band's *Kogun* by E. Taylor Atkins
S.O.B.'s *Don't Be Swindle* by Mahon Murphy and Ran Zwigenberg

Forthcoming Titles:
Kohaku Utagassen: The Red and White Song Contest by Shelley Brunt
Yellow Magic Orchestra's *Yellow Magic Orchestra* by Toshiyuki Ohwada

33 1/3 Brazil
Series Editor: Jason Stanyek
Covering the genres of samba, tropicália, rock, hip hop, forró, bossa nova, heavy metal and funk, among others, 33 1/3 Brazil is a series devoted to in-depth examination of the most important Brazilian albums of the twentieth and twenty-first centuries.

Published Titles:
Caetano Veloso's *A Foreign Sound* by Barbara Browning
Tim Maia's *Tim Maia Racional Vols. 1 &2* by Allen Thayer
João Gilberto and Stan Getz's *Getz/Gilberto* by Brian McCann
Gilberto Gil's *Refazenda* by Marc A. Hertzman
Dona Ivone Lara's *Sorriso Negro* by Mila Burns
Milton Nascimento and Lô Borges's *The Corner Club* by Jonathon Grasse
Racionais MCs' *Sobrevivendo no Inferno* by Derek Pardue
Naná Vasconcelos's *Saudades* by Daniel B. Sharp
Chico Buarque's First *Chico Buarque* by Charles A. Perrone

Forthcoming titles:
Jorge Ben Jor's *África Brasil* by Frederick J. Moehn

33 1/3 Europe
Series Editor: Fabian Holt
Spanning a range of artists and genres, 33 1/3 Europe offers engaging accounts of popular and culturally significant albums of Continental Europe and the North Atlantic from the twentieth and twenty-first centuries.

Published Titles:
Darkthrone's *A Blaze in the Northern Sky* by Ross Hagen
Ivo Papazov's *Balkanology* by Carol Silverman
Heiner Müller and Heiner Goebbels's *Wolokolamsker Chaussee* by Philip V. Bohlman
Modeselektor's *Happy Birthday!* by Sean Nye
Mercyful Fate's *Don't Break the Oath* by Henrik Marstal

Bea Playa's *I'll Be Your Plaything* by Anna Szemere and András Rónai
Various Artists' *DJs do Guetto* by Richard Elliott
Czesław Niemen's *Niemen Enigmatic* by Ewa Mazierska and Mariusz Gradowski
Massada's *Astaganaga* by Lutgard Mutsaers
Los Rodriguez's *Sin Documentos* by Fernán del Val and Héctor Fouce
Édith Piaf's *Récital 1961* by David Looseley
Nuovo Canzoniere Italiano's *Bella Ciao* by Jacopo Tomatis
Iannis Xenakis's *Persepolis* by Aram Yardumian
Vopli Vidopliassova's *Tantsi* by Maria Sonevytsky
Amália Rodrigues's *Amália at the Olympia* by Lila Ellen Gray
Ardit Gjebrea's *Projekt Jon* by Nicholas Tochka
Aqua's *Aquarium* by C.C. McKee
J.M.K.E.'s *To the Cold Land* by Brigitta Davidjants
Taco Hemingway's *Jarmark* by Kamila Rymajdo
Einstürzende Neubauten's *Kollaps* by Melle Jan Kromhout and Jan Nieuwenhuis
CCCP – FEDELI ALLA LINEA's *Affinità – Divergenze Fra il Compagno Togliatti e Noi* by Giacomo Bottà

Forthcoming Titles:
Silly's *Februar* by Michael Rauhut
Sigur Rós' *Ágætis Byrjun* by Tore Størvold

33 1/3 Oceania

Series Editors: Jon Stratton (senior editor) and Jon Dale (specializing in books on albums from Aotearoa/New Zealand)

Spanning a range of artists and genres from Australian Indigenous artists to Maori and Pasifika artists, from Aotearoa/New Zealand noise music to Australian rock, and including music from Papua and other Pacific islands, 33 1/3 Oceania offers exciting accounts of albums that illustrate the wide range of music made in the Oceania region.

Published Titles:
John Farnham's *Whispering Jack* by Graeme Turner
The Church's *Starfish* by Chris Gibson

Regurgitator's *Unit* by Lachlan Goold and Lauren Istvandity
Kylie Minogue's *Kylie* by Adrian Renzo and Liz Giuffre
Alastair Riddell's *Space Waltz* by Ian Chapman
Hunters & Collectors's *Human Frailty* by Jon Stratton
The Front Lawn's *Songs from the Front Lawn* by Matthew Bannister
Bic Runga's *Drive* by Henry Johnson
The Dead C's *Clyma est mort* by Darren Jorgensen
Ed Kuepper's *Honey Steel's Gold* by John Encarnacao
Chain's *Toward the Blues* by Peter Beilharz
Hilltop Hoods' *The Calling* by Dianne Rodger
Screamfeeder's *Kitten Licks* by Ben Green and Ian Rogers
The Clean's *Boodle Boodle Boodle* by Geoff Stahl
The Avalanches' *Since I Left You* by Charles Fairchild
John Sangster's *Lord of the Rings Vols. 1–3* by Bruce Johnson
Soundtrack from *Saturday Night Fever* by Clinton Walker
Eyeliner's *BUY NOW* by Michael Brown
TISM's *Machiavelli and the Four Seasons* by Tyler Jenke
Crowded House's *Together Alone* by Barnaby Smith
silverchair's *Frogstomp* by Jay Daniel Thompson
Various Artists' *Truckload of Sky: The Lost Songs of David McComb Vol. 1* by Glenn D'Cruz
Robert Forster's *Danger in the Past* by Patrick Chapman
Tame Impala's *Currents* by Alister Newstead

Forthcoming Titles:
The Triffids' *Born Sandy Devotional* by Christina Ballico
5MMM's *Compilation Album of Adelaide Bands 1980* by Collette Snowden
INXS' *Kick* by Lauren Moxey
Sunnyboys' *Sunnyboys* by Stephen Bruel
The La De Das' *The Happy Prince* by John Tebbutt
Gary Shearston's *Dingo* by Peter Mills
Kate Ceberano's *Brave* by Panizza Allmark
Dinah Lee's *Introducing Dinah Lee* by Kimberly Cannady
The Waifs' *Up All Night* by Rebecca Bennison
The Three Out's *Move* by James Gaunt

Split Enz' *Mental Notes* by Michael Lamb
Douglas Lilburn's *Complete Electro-Acoustic Works* by Bruce Russell
Savage Garden's *Affirmation* by Pat O'Grady
Dick Diver's *Calendar Days* by Mitch Ryan

33 1/3 South Asia

Series Editor: Natalie Sarrazin

From the films of Bollywood and Lollywood, to home-grown *bhangra* hip-hop, Hindu devotional pop and Sufi rock, Sri Lankan rap, Indo jazz and disco, new-wave electronica and diasporic Asian Underground scene, 33 1/3 South Asia takes readers on a sonically diverse journey through the most significant soundtracks and albums from the twentieth and twenty-first centuries.

Published Titles:
Dil Chahta Hai Soundtrack by Jayson Beaster-Jones
Lata Mangeshkar's *My Favourites, Volume 2* by Anirudha Bhattacharjee and Chandrashekhar Rao
Coke Studio (Season 14) by Rakae Rehman Jamil and Khadija Muzaffar

33 1/3 Africa

Series Editor: Michael Veal

33 1/3 Africa is a series of books on canonical, album-length works of African music including traditional music, experimental music, and, with particular emphasis, popular music. Academic and journalistic writing results in sophisticated, nuanced and accessible narratives on African music.

Published Title:
Fela Anikulapo-Kuti's *Sorrow Tears and Blood* by Stephanie Shonekan

Forthcoming Titles:
Cesária Évora's *Miss Perfumado* by Jacqueline Georgis
Paul Simon's *Graceland* by Kalvin Schmidt-Rimpler Dinh
Nico, Rochereau, Roger & L'African Fiesta – *Volume 1 (1962–1963)* by Frank Gunderson

Currents

Alister Newstead

Jon Stratton, UniSA Creative, University of South Australia, and
Jon Dale, University of Melbourne, Australia

BLOOMSBURY ACADEMIC
NEW YORK • LONDON • OXFORD • NEW DELHI • SYDNEY

BLOOMSBURY ACADEMIC

Bloomsbury Publishing Inc, 1359 Broadway, New York, NY 10018, USA
Bloomsbury Publishing Plc, 50 Bedford Square, London, WC1B 3DP, UK
Bloomsbury Publishing Ireland, 29 Earlsfort Terrace, Dublin 2, D02 AY28, Ireland

BLOOMSBURY, BLOOMSBURY ACADEMIC and the Diana logo are
trademarks of Bloomsbury Publishing Plc

First published in the United States of America 2026

Copyright © Alister Newstead, 2026

For legal purposes the Acknowledgements on pp. xi–xii constitute an
extension of this copyright page.

All rights reserved. No part of this publication may be: i) reproduced or
transmitted in any form, electronic or mechanical, including photocopying,
recording or by means of any information storage or retrieval system without
prior permission in writing from the publishers; or ii) used or reproduced in
any way for the training, development or operation of artificial intelligence (AI)
technologies, including generative AI technologies. The rights holders expressly
reserve this publication from the text and data mining exception as per Article
4(3) of the Digital Single Market Directive (EU) 2019/790.

Bloomsbury Publishing Inc does not have any control over, or responsibility
for, any third-party websites referred to or in this book. All internet addresses
given in this book were correct at the time of going to press. The author and
publisher regret any inconvenience caused if addresses have changed or sites
have ceased to exist, but can accept no responsibility for any such changes.

A catalog record for this book is available from the Library of Congress.

ISBN:		
	HB:	979-8-7651-3700-0
	PB:	979-8-7651-3701-7
	ePDF:	979-8-7651-3703-1
	eBook:	979-8-7651-3704-8

Series: 33 1/3 Oceania

Typeset by Integra Software Services Pvt. Ltd.
Printed and bound in the United States of America

For product safety related questions contact productsafety@bloomsbury.com.

To find out more about our authors and books visit www.bloomsbury.com
and sign up for our newsletters.

Contents

Acknowledgements xi
Preface xiii

Introduction 1
Why focus on *Currents*? 2
Diving into *Currents* 4
A decade-defining artist 7
'Did you know Tame Impala is actually just one guy?' 9
In this book … 12

1 **Past Life: A potted biography** 13

2 **Powerlines: The importance of Perth** 17
Perth and its music scene 17
The internet's impact on Perth 22
Troy Terrace 24
Debunking myths about Perth 27
Rejecting (and embracing) Perth's influence 32

3 **B.C. (Before *Currents*)** 37
Kevin Parker: Studio wizard 39

4 **'Yes I'm Changing': Track-by-track analysis** 43
Track 1. 'Let It Happen' 43
Track 2. 'Nangs' 49
Track 3. 'The Moment' 53
Track 4. 'Yes I'm Changing' 56
Track 5. 'Eventually' 59
Track 6. 'Gossip' 62

5   'Eventually': *Currents* as 'break-off' album 63
   Track 7. 'The Less I Know The Better' 64
   Track 8. 'Past Life' 68
   Track 9. 'Disciples' 71
   Track 10. ''Cause I'm A Man' 74
   Track 11. 'Reality In Motion' 78
   Track 12. 'Love/Paranoia' 80
   Track 13. 'New Person, Same Old Mistakes' 83

6   A.C. (After *Currents*) 89
   Disciples: Kevin Parker's internet fame 89
   Tame Impala's success on Spotify 93
   The vinyl revival 97
   'New Person, Same Old Mistakes': Kevin Parker's collaborations and influence 99
   The path to pop 101
   Tame Impala's influence on hip hop 102
   What *Currents* made possible 104

7   A few final thoughts 107

Notes 109
References 113
Index 133

Acknowledgements

First, I want to acknowledge this title was researched and written on the lands of the Wurundjeri Woi Wurrung people of the Kulin Nation, the traditional custodians of this land, which was never ceded. I want to recognize their enduring connection to Country and its songlines. Making, sharing, listening to and learning from music has long been the First Nations way of life, not merely history but a living practice. In that spirit, I hope to continue participating towards cultural memory.

A huge thanks to series editor, Jon Stratton, for supporting and encouraging me throughout the process, helping make a daunting task seem surmountable and always guided rather than pushed. You taught me that sometimes The Less I Write The Better.

Immeasurable love and gratitude to my darling chip, Anna, for your endless and enthusiastic support. You held space for what made this special when I'd lost sight of it. And to Leo, now we can catch up on lost Farm and Lego time. I hope you read this one day and feel proud, or better yet, nerd out on Tame Impala with me. Eventually.

Respect and gratitude to Dan Condon, Bhakthi Puvanenthiran and my work colleagues for encouraging and allowing me the headspace and time to pursue this project wholeheartedly.

Thanks to my friend and writing hero Sose Fuamoli for being among the first to dive into the developing currents. And to Tyler Jenke, for showing it can be done. And done well. I'd also like to acknowledge the ongoing inspiration of these writers and critics: Tom Breihan, Jessica Hopper, Steven Hyden, Craig Mathieson, Jon Parales, Ann Powers, Simon Reynolds and Laura Snapes.

I'm indebted to the Tame Impala fandom, particularly on r/tameimpala, and to all the journalists and writers whose many interviews and articles helped inform this book.

Lastly, infinite thanks to Kevin Parker for all the incredible, inspirational music. Looking forward to whatever you let happen next.

Preface

I didn't love Tame Impala instantly. I was a sceptic before I was a fan, a snob who dismissed them as 'Lame Impala'. But I realized the errors of my childish name calling, untangled my prejudices and rectified my incorrect opinion in time for the release of *Lonerism*. And then I was all in. Who wouldn't be? I've been a Tame Impala fan ever since and dutifully followed and covered Kevin Parker's career all those same years.

I'm not the type of disciple who'd die on a hill defending 'Wings of Time', for instance, but I am deeply suspicious of anyone who can't at least respect, if not admire Parker.

He could've made *Lonerism 2.0*, and it would've been great. He'd still be considered one of the most visionary and influential rock artists of his generation, coasting comfortably through mid-to-upper tiers of festivals for several more years. I suspect he even harboured some mixed feelings about *not* doing just that. Instead, Parker took a gamble with something more adventurous, questioning his own fundamentals regarding genre, taste and audiences.

He bet on *Currents,* a record that rattled fan expectations and conceptions. And yet, it's not an inherently challenging album, far from it. It's a well-considered and even-better-executed sonic evolution, not a knee-jerk reaction to fuzzy guitars. It shouldn't be thought of in terms of what Tame Impala wouldn't do but a horizon-expanding trek where Parker gave himself permission to entertain many possibilities. And found he could do many of them remarkably well.

I believe you can put *Currents* on at any time (right now, even!), and it has the potential to entice and bedazzle, sounding simultaneously cutting-edge and yet familiar, fashionably retro. The sense of past, present and future colliding that the music evokes is a vivid product of the 2010s, tangling itself in a web of influences from every other decade, even inspiring some still to come.

Tasking myself with writing one of (if not) the first books about Tame Impala, I certainly felt an instinct and some strange responsibility early on to write a biography. But realized, thanks to the already enlightened guidance of my editor, Jon, and partner, Anna, that this is not that book. It's a volume about *Currents*, the pivot point that made Tame Impala what it is today. And perhaps, vainly, a solid foundation for future writing and a full biography. (Kevin, my DMs are open!) If nothing else, my hope is this book will reach its intended audience. That it will reignite, or possibly spark, an esteem for Tame Impala and let those *Currents* take you where they may – to entertain, enlighten, furnish you with some newfound appreciation, with some enriching questions as much as answers.

Introduction

It is 9 March 2015. I'm roughly six months into a new role as Music News Producer at Australia's national youth broadcaster, triple j, and a bombshell is about to be dropped on me. My bosses have offered me a clandestine reveal: one of Australia's (and my personal) favourite artists is releasing the first track of their new album in the morning. Be prepared.

Mid-morning, 10 March 2015. Even after only a few listens – as many plays as this new song's nearly-eight-minute length would allow before deadline – I'm already confident I'm listening to the song of the year. 'Let It Happen', much like the highly anticipated third Tame Impala album it heralded, marked a drastic sonic departure from what had gone before. Where Tame Impala's previous albums, the critically acclaimed 2010 debut *InnerSpeaker* and equally revered 2012 follow-up *Lonerism*, welcomed comparisons to psych-rock forebears – 'John Lennon fronting Pink Floyd', for instance – 'Let It Happen' was a hard pivot towards new horizons. An expansive, shape-shifting voyage that sounded less like acid-rock epiphany and more like a cosmic, all-night rave, complete with synthesizers and mechanical beats sculpted for the dancefloor, the track polarized fans as much as it invited admiration for its bold new direction. It was a lot to take in one morning.

Nearly ten years later, however, I'm convinced 'Let It Happen' and parent album *Currents* is a game-changing masterpiece that contained several strokes of genius from West Australian artist Kevin Parker, the certified multi-hyphenate who writes, performs, records, self-produces and regularly mixes all of Tame Impala's music.

It's a fascinating narrative: the private, not-really-a-band project of an introverted stoner who became one of the defining Australian acts of his generation. Tame Impala's Kevin Parker not only reignited a love for psychedelic music at home and abroad but was critical in prompting renewed attention for Australian music overseas in the 2010s, alongside popular exports like electronic producer Flume, singer-songwriter Courtney Barnett and wig-wearing pop star Sia (Stratton, Dale and Mitchell 2020).

Aside from the strength of the music itself, Tame Impala's explosive popularity stems from a unique alchemy of timing, place, and a raft of parallel shifts in music consumption and the wider industry during the 2010s. Despite being widely revered as a seminal Australian act, there's a deficit of published literature dedicated to Tame Impala. This book aims to correct that.

Why focus on *Currents*?

There are many reasons to dedicate a volume in the 33⅓ Oceania series to Tame Impala. There're convincing cases to be mounted for *InnerSpeaker* or *Lonerism*, which established Parker's psych-rock artistry, pairing mind-melting production with singular songwriting, earning spots in 'Greatest Australian Albums' rankings. But *Currents*, released 17 July 2015, marks a major turning point in Parker's personal and professional life, after which nothing was the same.

A conscious shift in sound and attitude, *Currents* distanced Parker from the lo-fi sound of his earlier work. He embraced soul, disco, R&B, dance, funk and his latent pop instincts, doing for these genres what he arguably did with psych- and progressive rock: made them fashionable again by re-wiring the past into vivid, future-facing music.

True to its title, *Currents* flows – musically, lyrically and thematically – around metamorphosis. Across thirteen tracks, Parker reshapes Tame Impala by welcoming the new, both stylistically and personally. He's still grappling with the familiar neuroses that rattled around his head on *InnerSpeaker* and *Lonerism*, but also reckons with the life-altering impacts of tortured romance and his ballooning fame, often simultaneously. That transformation is telegraphed in song titles like 'Let It Happen' and 'The Moment'. Or more explicitly, 'Yes, I'm Changing' and 'New Person, Same Old Mistakes'.

This evolution is paralleled in the sound – Parker's signature introspection framed in brighter, more polished and danceable contexts. Emboldened by growing confidence and new studio equipment, Parker infused the album with vibrant colour and clarity that's more in conversation with contemporary pop, hip hop and electronic music, without sacrificing Tame Impala's spirit and compositional DNA.

Currents was a risk, but the rewarding result? Tame Impala's best-selling album, breaking through to a bigger, broader audience. It reached #1 on the Australian charts for the first time, #3 in the United Kingdom and #4 in the United States, earning Platinum sales in six countries (Australia, Denmark, New Zealand, Poland, the United Kingdom and the United States), transforming the group into festival-headlining Gen Z idols. *Currents* expanded Tame Impala's appeal as exquisitely woozy music ready-made for escapism (or getting high to), immersive enough for private headphone listening yet with enough stadium-sized sensibilities to enjoy with thousands of fans in packed arenas and festivals.

Tame Impala had experienced industry adulation before but *Currents* won five Australian Recording Industry Association (ARIA) Awards, including Album of the Year, Best Rock Album, and Best Group (the same three Tame Impala won in 2013). Parker also took home Producer of the Year and Engineer of the Year. 'Let It Happen' won the Song of the Year at the 2016 Australasian Performing Right Association (APRA) Awards, Tame Impala took home Best International Group at the 2016 BRIT Awards and *Currents* also earned Parker a second Grammy nomination for Best Alternative Music Album.

The album's enduring critical prestige includes ranking in *Rolling Stone*'s 500 Greatest Albums of All Time (at #382) and the Australian edition's 200 Greatest Australian Albums (at #12). And as the record neared its tenth anniversary, its impact and importance steadily grew.

Diving into *Currents*

The album's transformative journey begins with its lead single, opening track and prophetic statement of purpose, 'Let It Happen'. Fusing the pulse of pop and electronic dance music with the psychedelic zeal Parker had arguably already perfected, it's a tsunami of urgent synths, drums and tumbling counter-melodies, all propelled forward by insistent rhythmic drive and a compelling lyrical narrative. *'It's always around me, all this noise'*, Parker intones. *'Not nearly as loud as the voice saying "Let it happen, let it happen"'*. The words immediately invite intrigue, and the kaleidoscopic odyssey that follows reveals a synthesis of melancholy and ecstasy, capturing the equally thrilling and terrifying experience of transformation.

Halfway through, there's the inspirational moment where the track appears to malfunction, skipping like a scratched CD. Who'd think to derail their own momentum with an obstacle like that? Someone able to stylishly reset the song's groove, diverting its flow towards a vivid, panoramic climax.

In the closing moments, a poly-voiced Parker mumbles self-motivations against a sawing guitar riff (made all the more gratifying by its delayed arrival). The textures cascade and coalesce into a transcendental vamp that drifts off into neon-lit infinity, as if we've heard just part of an ongoing alien transmission. That's almost more plausible than the reality: 'Let It Happen' was conceived and executed by one man between globetrotting recording sessions and his home in Fremantle, Western Australia.

That's ultimately why 'Let It Happen' feels as revelatory on the hundredth spin as it does the first. Beneath its ambitious, borderless sound lies a deeply human intimacy. The sound of an individual, albeit a super-talented one, scrutinizing themself, grappling with their anxieties and limitations – and deciding to let go, to let the *Currents* pull them where they may. In the song's closing moments, Parker sings in searching falsetto:

'Oh, I'm ready for the moment and the sound
Oh, but maybe I was ready all along'

That epiphany is rendered – unwittingly, or perhaps subversively – as Parker's way of preparing us for what's to come. Yet, nobody could've predicted how 'Let It Happen' marked the beginning of a significant new chapter.

You know who else felt that way about 'Let It Happen'? Daniel Johns. 'That shit fucked me up,' the Silverchair frontman told Parker in an episode of his Spotify podcast.

> When that came out, I remember just going 'Oh, shit, the game's changed'. I thought it was such a bold artistic move. The first single goes for [seven] and a half minutes … It's so punk and progressive. I thought it was a wonderful choice.
>
> (*Who Is Daniel Johns?* 2021)

It's an intimate exchange that scans as a passing of the torch moment. Fronting Silverchair, one of Australia's most commercially successful musical exports, Johns evolved over five albums and profoundly shaped the Australian music scene. He went from teenage grunge rock prodigy in the 1990s (detailed in Jay Daniel Thompson's 33⅓ Oceania title on *Frogstomp*) into a composer of artsy, aspirational music ripe with theatrical flair and boundary-testing ambition.

Like many kids of the 1990s, Parker strongly identified with Silverchair, first falling in love after his older brother introduced him to their second album, 1997's *Freak Show*. 'It was super grunge,' as he told *NME*. 'They just had this fucking attitude: just three longhaired dudes slaying their instruments – headbanging and shouting' (Cooper 2015). After hearing 'Freak', Parker wanted to start his own band. 'They were quite young Australian dudes. "It's not on the other side of the world, it's on the other side of the country, and they're only a little bit older than me – so if I work hard now, I can get where they are by the time I'm 15!" I was 11 or 12' (Cooper 2015).

I'd submit Kevin Parker and Tame Impala took up Johns' mantle, mirroring his evolution and impact into the 2010s and beyond, becoming the decade's equivalent of Silverchair: an internationally renowned Australian act driven by a singular creative auteur.

A decade-defining artist

Tame Impala's 2010 debut album *InnerSpeaker* reached back and lifted from late 1960s and 1970s rock band playbooks, fusing hazy, expansive arrangements with stoner-friendly riffs and textures. You could hear Parker channelling plenty of late-period Beatles, blues-rockers Cream and Blue Cheer, and one of his biggest influences, Swedish psych-rockers Dungen. But beneath the crunchy, guitar-driven sagas were Parker's deeply personal neuroses and love of seclusion. *'There's a party in my head and no one is invited'* he sang on breakout single 'Solitude Is Bliss'. Self-doubt and isolation rarely sounded so great.

On 2012 follow-up *Lonerism*, Parker's sound developed into something more widescreen, drawing kaleidoscopic production and songwriting inspiration from the 1970s output of Todd Rundgren and Supertramp, and layering it against 'really cheesy pop melodies' (Reese 2012). Parker likened the results to 'Britney Spears singing with The Flaming Lips' (Fink 2012). Buoyed by hit singles 'Elephant' and 'Feels Like We Only Go Backwards', *Lonerism* felt beamed in from a bygone era yet resonated deeply with a younger audience keenly attuned to the crippling feelings of alienation and ambivalence of their increasingly online existence (Lohkamp 2023).

By 2015, however, Parker began to resist his 'psych-rock saviour' mantle (Newstead 2020a; Zammitt 2015). *Currents* was fashionably *un*-rock, a break from his previous records that stripped away the overblown amps, stretches of jam-band noodling and fuzzy shroud around his vocals – a reedy baritone that's endlessly (and justifiably) compared to John Lennon. In their place, was something cleaner, more immediate and unapologetically pleasurable.

'I've always liked pop music. I love what it does to my brain, and I've shut it out for a long time,' Parker reflected. 'The more I question myself about why I think pop is taboo, the more I realize it's not' (Hyden 2015). That revelation was liberating for Parker, who'd developed complicated genre prejudices growing up in the 1990s. He identified as a grunge, alt-rock and punk loving teen but was drawn to pop, electronic, dance and R&B – genres historically seen in opposition to guitar-based music. They were 'separate camps, you could only be one side or the other', he explained (Beta 2015).

The songs on *Currents* weren't built for radio and the charts, but they borrowed the glossy vernacular of music with broad appeal. There's silky R&B, funk's buttery bottom-end and rhythmic snap, glittery disco, soft rock balladry, cosmic power pop, synth-laden chill out music – all given Parker's signature lysergic soak. The type of music he'd previously struggled pursuing for fear 'indie-music snobs would turn their nose[s] up at it' (Hyden 2015). But *Currents* demonstrated his natural gift for infectious yet emotionally resonant ear candy that was still unmistakably Tame Impala. He didn't abandon mind-altering soundscapes or his commitment to reimagining the past to divine a musical future, but his lodestar now twinkled with visions of *Thriller*-era Michael Jackson, Bee Gees, Stevie Wonder, Fleetwood Mac, Daft Punk, Air, Goa beach raves and beyond. 'I wanted to make weird pop music, and I wasn't afraid [to] stand behind it,' Parker told *NME* for the album's fifth anniversary (Smith 2020). He knew *Currents* could divide fans 'because they've got their values set. But if I can convince a few die-hard rock fans that '80s synths can fit over a '70s drum beat – if I can help them to look outside the square of traditional psych-rock – then at least one mission is accomplished' (Goble 2015).

Currents reflected its creator's personal music revolution, but also broader shifts in the 2010s music landscape, particularly the impact of streaming services. Subscription-based platforms like Spotify, Apple Music, TIDAL and YouTube Music revolutionized the industry, overtaking physical media (CDs, vinyl, cassettes) and paid digital downloads (largely from iTunes) as the dominant source of everyday music consumption (Arditi 2018: 302). Giving users easy access to a vast musical history, streaming made the crossover between mainstream hits and obscurities inevitable, altering listening habits and making the boundaries separating genres and eras less distinctive. This represented a revolution for so many music obsessives just like Parker:

> Where I used to have to walk to a music shop and physically go to the dance section feeling embarrassed about looking at house music when I was a kid, now I can just visit Spotify and you can immediately listen. Everything's available to you, which is great. Things are less distant and foreign than they used to be.
>
> (Jenkins 2020)

Currents embodied and possibly even encouraged this increasingly open-eared musical attitude, riding the waves from this significant change to great success. Its masterful drift between styles and moods presaged the genre-agnostic attitude that would come to typify 2010s popular music, blurring the boundaries between genres, sounds and even the roles of solo producer and band.

'Did you know Tame Impala is actually just one guy?'

Before continuing, we must address a key distinction: Tame Impala is the solo project of Kevin Parker. He's a multi-instrumentalist studio prodigy, like Prince and Stevie Wonder, but Tame Impala also exists as a live band. It's a situation relatively common in the worlds of alt-rock and indie music. Think of Trent Reznor and Nine Inch Nails, Dave Grohl and Foo Fighters, Justin Vernon and Bon Iver – projects whose frontmen maintain their status as primary creative auteur amid evolving touring ensembles.

'Tame Impala has two lives,' Parker once told *The NZ Herald* (Taylor 2016). 'One is the album, which is like a producer, and the other life is like a band. More of a live incarnation where we're basically a covers band for the albums that I produce.' Over time, this unique aspect became a joke among Parker's legion of admirers. 'Did you know Tame Impala is actually just one guy?' grew into a well-known quip – mocking music trivia nerds mansplaining an obvious fact. Before it became common knowledge in the early 2020s (the phrase's precise origins, like most internet memes, is fuzzy), the fact Tame Impala *is* Kevin Parker was an understandable source of confusion. Parker's music sounds like a band and presents as such on stage, with a line-up of close friends and long-time collaborators. Originally, the touring band comprised Parker, guitarist Dom Simper, drummer Jay Watson and bassist Nick Allbrook. After Allbrook's departure in 2013, Cameron Avery joined on bass, Watson shifted to keys and Julien Barbagallo took over drums.

In Tame Impala's early days, Parker actively encouraged the misconception it was a band and not a solo project. When he signed to hip independent label Modular Recordings in 2008, he sheepishly presented Tame Impala as a trio rather than his own multi-tracked home recordings. 'I outright lied to them,' he confessed to producer Rick Rubin on the *Broken Record* podcast:

> The contract we signed was for three of us … Because I didn't want to say it was just me, for a number of reasons. Number one, I was kind of shy. It's really weird because looking back, it's like, 'why the fuck didn't you just own it?' But also, the [Perth] music scene I was in was a very communal scene … For the thing that finally came out of that scene to be a solo project? It felt kind of wrong.
>
> (Broken Record 2020)

Currents marked a course correction in Tame Impala's perception. Publicity for the album focused solely on Parker, breaking from seven years of press photos and interviews featuring his bandmates, solidifying him as chief auteur. A pivotal moment that cemented Parker's graduation from introverted studio hermit into Australia's most unlikely pop star.

A leader, not a follower, *Currents* positioned Parker as a self-sustaining creative force, transforming him into an in-demand collaborator. In the years that followed, his reputation and influence spread through substantial songwriting and production credits. His star-studded resume spanned **deep breath** pop stars (Lady Gaga, Dua Lipa, The Weeknd); rap elite (Travis Scott, Kendrick Lamar, Kanye West); icons (Mick Jagger, Diana Ross), as well as taste-makers like SZA, Gorillaz, Kali Uchis, The Streets, Miguel, Justice, and even iconic children's act The Wiggles! (We'll dive into this and more in Chapter 6).

Not bad for a shy, shaggy teen that once played gigs with a towel draped over his head. Nobody could've predicted that the reticent teen lurking in Perth venue basements would become one of modern music's most celebrated and sought-after sonic architects, setting trends rather than chasing them. The former astronomy student using sounds of the past to map constellations of where music could be heading.

In this book ...

The forthcoming chapters, some named after songs from *Currents*, will consider the album from various perspectives. Chapter 1, 'Past Life', provides a biography of Kevin Parker and how Tame Impala developed. Chapter 2, 'Powerlines', focuses on Perth and how its historical, cultural and social contexts influenced Parker's artistic development and identity. Chapter 3, 'B.C. (Before *Currents*)', details the lead-up to the album. Chapters 4 and 5 ('Yes I'm Changing' and 'Eventually') offer a track-by-track breakdown, analysing sound, lyrics, composition, production and themes, and also interpreting *Currents* as a break-up album through biographical elements. Chapter 6, 'A.C. (After *Currents*)', explores everything that happened after the album's release. We'll examine its importance as a decade-defining release that reflected drastic cultural, musical and technological shifts of the 2010s. In addition we will explore Tame Impala's relationship with internet fandom and Parker's post-*Currents* career as a sought-after producer, songwriter and collaborator. That will bring us to present day and final reflection on an album that Tame Impala devotees (like you, like me) hold dear.

Having offered the divisions of 'Before *Currents*' and 'After *Currents*', here in 10 A.C. (that's the year 2025), *Currents* can be viewed as a cultural landmark in contemporary Australian music. The record by which Tame Impala, and the countless acts and imitators that rose in its wake, is measured.

1 Past Life: A potted biography

Talented yet often self-deprecating, Kevin Parker is full of fascinating contradictions. An in-demand collaborator at his most creative when working alone. A perfectionist who swears by spontaneity. A self-confessed loner who comfortably performs in front of thousands. To better understand these contradictions, we must go back to the beginning.

Born on 20 January 1986, to his South African mother, Rosalind, and Jerry, an Zimbabwean accountant, Kevin moved with his family to the West Australian outback town of Kalgoorlie at age three when his father became CFO of mining company Gold Fields. A year later, Kevin's parents divorced, and he grew up shuttling between homes in WA's capital city, Perth: with his mother in middle-class Mt. Lawley, and upper-middle-class Cottesloe, with his father, older brother Steve and stepmother Rhonda. At age 15, Kevin's parents briefly reunited, only to split again. 'The first 17 years of my life, my family life, were like a soap opera,' Parker reflected. 'And I just got closed off' (Janssen 2017).

He was a 'sensitive kid ... Maybe because I didn't have that solid foundation beneath me' (Weiner 2019), and developed a near-chronic shyness. 'From an early age, I found being alone incredibly liberating. As a teenager ... I'd get very frustrated because I was never comfortable in social situations. Once I finished school, I was like, "Well, fuck it. I'm done with people"' (Jones 2015).

Music became Parker's refuge, and learning drums at age 10 gave him a profound sense of identity (Newstead 2015). His father, who played in cover bands, was a crucial influence, teaching his son guitar and introducing him to a treasure trove of vinyl that shaped his son's tastes – The Beatles, Supertramp, Beach Boys and The Shadows. At 12, Kevin began experimenting with his father's two-track tape recorders, looping himself on drums and layering over vocals, guitar or keys to create 'weird, genreless, almost-electronic songs' (Fink 2015a). Those production fundamentals would end up serving him his entire career. 'I just thought it was crazy that I was jamming with myself! It blew my mind' (Janssen 2017). For the introverted child of divorce, music offered solace and a way to express emotions he couldn't share elsewhere.

> I could just completely open up ... because I never really talked about my problems with anyone. Especially in high school I was a pretty closed off kid, so when I discovered this outlet, I could really bare my soul.
>
> (Fink 2015a)

Using an eight-track recorder gifted to him at 16, Parker became obsessed but kept his 'unlistenable' recordings private for many years (Douris 2021). One of the first to hear them was Dominic Simper, a close friend and future bandmate. The pair met in Year 9 at John XXIII College – an expensive Catholic private school in Mount Claremont – bonding as the only music lovers in a sport-obsessed environment. 'Perth is the kind of place where if you're Mozart, you'd play someone a song and they'd shrug their shoulders and go back to talking about football,' Simper recalled (Fink 2015a). Parker added: 'We instantly bonded [once] I got over my jealousy of him being a better guitarist than me ... I'd show him my songs [and] trust that he'll give me a brutally honest opinion' (Janssen 2017).

Simper joined Parker's first band The Dee Dee Dums, founded in 2004 alongside friend Luke Epstein. Inspired by Hendrix, Led Zeppelin and 2000s Australian rockers Wolfmother, the group played riff-heavy blues rock and gained local attention through gigs and 'battle of the bands' competitions.

After school, Parker enrolled in mining engineering at the Curtin University of Technology to please his 'success-and-academia driven' father, who discouraged a career in music (Douris 2021). Parker switched to civil engineering, then a degree in astronomy, a childhood interest.[1] He had 'submitted to the reality that I wasn't actually going to be a famous musician' (Blanchard 2010). But music never left Parker's mind. 'It was a disease. I would not be able to listen to a word in lectures because I'd just be thinking about my new song' (Blanchard 2010).

In 2005, Parker met Nick Allbrook at the AmpFest: Clash of the Bands, where The Dee Dee Dums came second to Allbrook's band, Electric Blue Acid Dogs. Soon after, the Dogs rechristened to Mink Mussel Creek and recruited Parker on drums. By 2006, they were being managed by Jodie Regan, who was at the time running new Fremantle venue The Norfolk Basement, which became the band's 'second home'. Parker routinely used the space to record drums for his own music (Lawrie and Moodie 2018). Allbrook later noticed a 'seismic shift' in Parker's music towards a 'blissed-out, pretty melody, [and] psychedelic' sound (Noisevox 2010).

The Dee Dee Dums morphed into Tame Impala and debuted at Fremantle live music institution Mojos Bar (Lawrie and Moodie 2018) just months after recruiting sixteen-year-old Jay Watson on drums. '[He was] sleeping on the couch at Troy Terrace, which is where Kevin and ["Shiny" Joe Ryan] lived,' recalled Regan. 'And Nick was in the garden shed out the back' (Levin 2018).

Regan began managing Tame Impala and, when Mink Mussel Creek dissolved, also took on Pond – co-founded in 2008 by Allbrook, Watson and Ryan (who'd each develop solo projects). Pond released three home-recorded albums before gaining wider attention with 2012's *Beard, Wives, Denim*, produced by Parker, who drummed for the group between 2009 and 2011. 'It was really very organic,' said Regan. 'They all still play together, record together, hang out together. It really hasn't changed very much from those early days' (Levin 2018). This collective looked up to Regan as 'this buffer between us and the outside world' (Brown 2020), and helped Parker's shyness in promoting Tame Impala.

> I was never going to be one of those artists that's fully independent, shopping music around. I never sent my demos to a single record label … I assumed my music was going to be for me and my friends, unless a record label found it.
>
> (Douris 2021)

That's precisely what happened when Glen Goetze, then A&R manager for Sydney label Modular, discovered Tame Impala on MySpace and loved what he heard.[2] A Universal Music Australian imprint founded in 1998, Modular was considered one of Australia's hippest labels, boasting acts like Wolfmother, The Avalanches, The Presets and Perth's Eskimo Joe. Parker remembers Goetze calling with an offer to fly Tame Impala to Sydney for a showcase and sign them just before his final astronomy exam:

> I was walking around uni, the exam was in 20 minutes and I was meant to be studying but I was thinking about this call … [It] came on the way there and I was like, 'Fuck it, sweet! I'm out!' After that I drove home to our share house and told Jay [Watson].
>
> (Smith 2015)

2 Powerlines: The importance of Perth

Tame Impala is arguably Perth's most famous music export, and yet Parker's relationship to his hometown is ambivalent and nuanced, rejecting the idea of it being integral to his artistic identity, or even influential to his music. He's suggested not feeling a connection to Perth's rich musical history or unique local scene outside of a close circle of friends he came up with. And yet, he's also occasionally conceded to the importance of his Perth roots. Regardless of Parker's perspective, I'd argue Perth plays an undeniable influence on Tame Impala with discernible links to the city's music history, which has been shaped by Perth's unique characteristics.

Perth and its music scene

Western Australia's capital city, Perth, is located 4,000km west of Australia's largest cities, Sydney and Melbourne. As such, as David Whish-Wilson writes in his book on the city:

> Perth is often described as the world's most isolated capital city. It's a title less relevant than it was for most of the twentieth century, when flying interstate was expensive and the Nullarbor Plain was crossed via a dirt track.
>
> (2013: 12)

Honolulu actually holds the title of 'most isolated capital city', with Perth closer to Indonesia and Singapore than

Australia's eastern cities. However, Perth's relative distance from the rest of Australia means its remoteness remains a deeply ingrained 'aspect that has characterised its sense of identity from settlement to the present' (Trainer 2016: 101). Besides its relative isolation from the east coast, gifting Perth a certain self-sufficiency and sense of innovation, another of the defining ways in which Perth is regularly perceived and discussed is its suburban nature. Unlike other Australian cities, Perth was settled later, in 1829, and had a slower population increase. Historian Jenny Gregory writes that 'Perth's suburbs developed rapidly in the 1920s, fed by immigration from Britain and natural population growth, and shaped by new tramways, bus routes and the motor car' (Gregory 2003: 7). This resulted in Perth lacking the nineteenth-century terrace houses, corner shops and local pubs that define the condensed inner city areas of other Australian cities (Howe 1994).

Instead, urban development focused on spreading outwards from Perth's relatively small urban centre. Fuelled by a post-war economic boom, the 1950s were a period of rapid expansion, catering to further population growth by extending into the vast lands available along the coast. As a result, Perth's metropolitan area spans almost 6,500km^2, a largely middle-class suburban sprawl. Today, it stretches almost 150 km along the coast, north from Two Rocks down south to Mandurah,[1] framed by the Indian Ocean to the west and the expansive agricultural Wheatbelt region to the east. Perth has also benefitted from an affluent economy, underpinned by a history of boom and bust cycles driven by resource mining, from the late nineteenth-century gold rush to the 2000s surge in iron ore, coal and other minerals in northern WA[2] (Phillips 2016).

Despite Perth's size and population of 2.17 million (just behind Sydney, Melbourne and Brisbane), it retains a perception as a small, insular city boasting a laid-back lifestyle, punctuated by its many beaches, parks and a pleasant, regularly sunny climate. Parker has described Perth as 'a place with Los Angeles' scenery, but a small rural town's mindset' (Brown 2020). Consequently, a long-held myth shaping the Perth experience is it being a 'clean, overregulated and sprawling suburban city with little in the way of urban space, or the cultural life that comes with its requisite density and diversity' as Adam Trainer noted researching the development of Perth's punk scene from the 1970s (Trainer 2016: 101).

Perth's unique characteristics – its relative isolation, suburban nature and a 'small town' mentality – are defining qualities impacting its music scene. Academics like Trainer, Jon Stratton (2007, 2008), Tara Brabazon (2005) and Christina Ballico (2012, 2013) have examined how Perth's historical lack of a thriving inner city culture and music industry, combined with the distance from the interconnected east coast music scenes, fostered unique punk and alternative rock scenes. Through the late 1970s and 1980s, the lack of national attention and the prohibitive cost of interstate touring meant that besides a few exceptions (such as The Triffids, The Stems or Dave Warner's From The Suburbs) Perth musicians routinely left the city for the eastern states to 'make it' in music. This includes The Farriss Brothers (who relocated to Sydney and became INXS), Dave Faulkner (of Hoodoo Gurus and formerly The Victims), Kim Salmon (of The Scientists and The Cheap Nasties), Suze DiMarchi (of Baby Animals fame) and more.

This 'exodus of musicians and other creatives, mostly to Melbourne and Sydney, persisted as a constant drain on the city's cultural profile' (Stratton and Trainer 2016: 47). However, this situation shifted dramatically from the late 1990s, when Perth bands began finding recognition and success on a national, and sometimes international, level as part of Australia's 'alt rock' boom. As Craig Mathieson's book *The Sell-In* (2000) chronicles, this fertile but cutthroat period saw the local industry, inspired by the success of grunge, turning to focus on independent music and youth-oriented trends. This paved the way for Australian 'alt rock', which swiftly became a catch-all term for music that rejected pop and the mainstream. Ironically, through the 1990s (and well beyond) 'alternative' became a genre as dominant and commercial as the so-called mainstream it originally defined itself against.

This 'alt rock' boom period coincided with two major developments in the Australian music landscape. First, the Big Day Out grew from a Sydney-based music festival into a national touring event (Mathieson 2000), which more broadly, along with cheaper airfares, further enabled Perth venues to form part of touring circuits for national and international acts (Ballico 2013). Secondly, the nationalization of government-funded youth radio network triple j. Launched in 1975 as Double Jay, and limited to broadcasting in Sydney on AM, the network moved to FM in 1980 and rebranded to triple j before broadcasting nationally in 1989 (Collins 2015). As part of the ABC, triple j rejected commercial radio's ideologies and programming, increasingly platforming 'alternative' music through the 1990s, making a point to feature acts from underrepresented scenes across Australia. The expansion of radio and festivals, along with TV and street press, enriched Australia's music scene, allowing acts to reach audiences nationwide and strengthened local scenes, regardless of location.

These changes had a critical effect on Perth, and the more bands remained in the city and successfully engaged with a national market, the more attitudes shifted towards Perth being a viable base to build and sustain a music career. Ballico calls this shift 'one of the most significant developments occurring in the [Perth] music industry between 1998–2009', while the nationalization of triple j and Big Day Out 'influenced not only the music which Perth musicians were exposed to but also supported the ability of the Perth music scene to connect with national audiences' (2013).

We can chart the growing popularity of nationally recognized and successful Perth artists by their ranking in triple j's Hottest 100, an annual countdown of the past year's favourite songs as voted by listeners. Between 1989 and 1997, only two Perth bands charted, The Triffids and Ammonia,[3] but representation grew exponentially after Jebediah charted three songs in 1998, including 'Harpoon' at #7. It kickstarted a trend of WA artists punching above their weight in the Hottest 100, regularly reaching (or debuting) in the top 10 into the 2000s and beyond. This included Eskimo Joe, The Sleepy Jackson (featuring Luke Steele, later of Empire of the Sun fame), End of Fashion, John Butler Trio, Little Birdy, Albany-bred The Waifs and rapper Drapht. WA representation peaked in 2004, with fourteen songs making the list, including three in the top 10.[4]

Tame Impala debuted in triple j's Hottest 100 in 2008, at #75 with 'Half Full Glass Of Wine'. The track's woolly, blues-rock riffs shared little with popular WA acts of the era, at odds with the arena-ready Birds of Tokyo or radio-friendly pop-rock of Eskimo Joe, Little Birdy and The Panics, let alone the rootsy folk of John Butler Trio and The Waifs. What Parker did have in common with these acts, however, was the sense of community he'd develop amid the city's relatively small music sector, and the role the internet played in significantly shaping Perth music through the 2000s.

The internet's impact on Perth

There's no overstating how much the near-ubiquitous uptake of the internet revolutionized the music industry worldwide. Perth was no exception. The advent of hugely popular social media service MySpace, started in August 2003, and respective audio and video sharing websites Soundcloud and YouTube, allowed musicians to independently share their music online, available to hear or download within a few clicks. Meanwhile, platforms like Facebook and Twitter enabled community updates on gigs and music, as well as direct communication with followers. Online music blogs also played a key role, with the inflating 2000s 'blogosphere' culture hyping up or dismissing the 'next big thing', boosting profiles of acts from anywhere on the planet, increasing demand but also accelerating turnover of new music. As WA journalist Simon Collins notes in 2009 Perth music documentary *Something in the Water*:

> There's no barrier now between recording a song and getting it on the internet or in a form where people can hear it. The internet and technology has meant that, while we don't have an advantage over any other states, we don't have that disadvantage any more.

(O'Bryan 2009)

Perth's mythic isolation was now essentially a moot point. Where bands had historically struggled to develop careers unless departing for elsewhere, Perth acts could now easily promote and distribute their music beyond WA's borders without leaving. The most immediate and obvious impact this had for Kevin Parker was his signing to Modular after Tame Impala's demos were discovered on MySpace. The internet also fostered a DIY ethos, which along with technological advances making home recording equipment cheaper and easier to use, meant Perth bands of the late 1990s and 2000s developed what Ballico identified as a 'largely self-sustaining local industry' with a 'strong work ethic' (Ballico 2012: 147) who routinely shared resources and supported each other. She details:

> Of particular interest was the fact that many of the musicians worked together on their recordings, collaborated between bands and albums, and went on tour together. Such networks had been formed through the relative isolation of Perth's scene and the concentration of limited but vibrant musical outlets, allowing the musicians to be creating, performing and recording in the same rehearsal spaces, live venues and recording studios. Coupled with a network of like minded people and long standing friendships, this helped foster and support music activity in Perth and give it a particular energy.
>
> (Ballico 2012: 44)

This 'energy' has been variously described as a 'family vibe' (by Panda Band's David Namour in Ballico 2012: 68), a 'special bond' (by Gyroscope's Rob Nassif in O'Bryan 2009), or as Jebediah frontman Kevin Mitchell deadpanned, 'very incestuous'[5] (O'Bryan 2009). This interconnected community is a result of the self-sufficiency fostered by Perth's distance from the east coast music industry.

Speaking on this collaborative network, Eskimo Joe guitarist Stu MacLeod notes how 'all the bands we've been surrounded by and been friends with have all had a passion for home recording' (O'Bryan 2009). Similarly, Eskimo Joe frontman Kav Temperly has said that 'jamming' informally with fellow musicians at home was 'a much bigger part of the scene' for him than gigging locally:

> It kind of peaked I guess in the mid-2000s. We had this killer jam room with myself and one of my partners in crime for years, a guy called Rodney Aravena, who played in End of Fashion and The Sleepy Jackson. That's where bands like Little Birdy and The Sleepy Jackson, Gyroscope, lots of bands came out and did their first demos. That was what my generation was about. It was about this bedroom-recording thing […] For me, that's the heart of where all of this stuff stems from – people connecting.
>
> (Lawrie and Moodie 2018)

Tame Impala weren't directly connected to this mid-2000s scene, but bedroom recording and 'people connecting' were crucial to Kevin Parker's early career and creativity, most evidently in his university days living with a group of 'muso' friends who together cultivated their own thriving, self-sufficient scene.

Troy Terrace

Struggling at university, Parker began skipping most classes and spending more time with a new set of friends who shared his musical obsession. He'd moved into a share house at 46 Troy Terrace in the spacious, leafy suburb of Daglish, situated in close proximity to the CBD by public transport. Adjacent to the affluent, inner-west suburb of Subiaco and dominated by parks and greenery, Daglish retains many of the original, low-cost homes constructed in the 1930s for working families (City of Subiaco 2023a, 2023b). The 2006 census found Daglish was largely a residential neighbourhood, which made 46 Troy Terrace an anomaly: a two-storey, semi-detached townhouse built in 1984 and occupied in the mid-2000s by Parker and his mates.

Instruments, amps, recording gear, and the scent of booze and weed filled every room, with vintage psychedelic music being a frequent soundtrack. 'We were totally those pot-smoking dropouts, listening to Jefferson Airplane and The Doors,' Parker recalls (Greenhaus 2015). In his bedroom upstairs, Parker privately recorded music inspired by 1960s rock bands (Cream, Jefferson Airplane), obscure krautrock and prog acts (like Demon Fuzz and Brainticket) and The Beatles' vocal melodies (Lodown 2009). 'We look back on Troy Terrace so romantically now but we lived in fucking squalor. I can smell it now,' Parker says.[6] 'I loved it there. It was the most creative environment I'd ever lived in' (Jones 2015).

Parker still considered his solo work as 'just one sliver of the giant amount of noise-making' (Mathieson 2010) he did with his housemates: Nick Allbrook, 'Shiny' Joe Ryan and Jay Watson. 'We all had like 10 bands we were in, usually at the same time' (Jones 2015). That complicated web included The Dee Dee Dums, short-lived psych-funk band Space Lime Peacock and Mink Mussel Creek, who splintered into Pond.

This melting pot of musos benefitted from Perth's relatively small yet highly concentrated live music sector. They'd spend weekends drinking and getting stoned before heading out for a gig (or several), playing house parties, garages, pubs in neighbouring Subiaco, or frequenting Fremantle venues including The Swan Basement, The Railway Hotel, The Newport Hotel, Fly By Night, Mojos Bar and The Norfolk Basement. 'I just felt such a sense of belonging. A newfound identity,' Parker recalled. 'It was such an intoxicating environment, the absolute tunnel vision of the music. It was the centre of how we lived our lives. Everything was based around that' (Lawrie and Moodie 2018).

This period of incessant gigging, communal jamming and bedroom recording mirrors the 'self-sustaining … strong work ethic' Ballico identified from the wave of 2000s Perth bands. However, the psych-rock racket Parker and his friends were making had little in common with the popular alt-rock Perth acts at the time. But then getting noticed wasn't their aim. 'Our attitude was, we are doing what we are doing because we love doing it. We're not out for approval or validation' (Lawrie and Moodie 2018). Prizing creative experimentation over commercial success, Parker and co. benefitted from what so many young musicians growing up in Perth had found advantageous: developing their sound and performance skills far from the prying eyes and ears of the major label 'power bases' of Melbourne and Sydney (Brabazon 2005: 4).

Bands like Eskimo Joe, Jebediah, End of Fashion and many more have expressed similar advantages (in *Something in the Water* and research from Ballico 2012). Similarly, Jodie Regan, long-time manager for Tame Impala, Pond and their various offshoots, calls Perth's isolation and lack of heavy industry presence a 'real blessing' for artistic development. 'Playing a gig, [you know] there's gonna be no label people, or record/music industry, or journalists … So you can do literally whatever the hell you want, until you work out what it is that you are gonna do' (Levin 2018).

This low-stakes environment permitted Parker and co. to foster an artistic identity and independence with little risk of embarrassment, pressure or exposure to the mainstream. Nick Allbrook would agree. In his essay *Creative Darwinism*,[7] Parker's close friend and collaborator writes:

> Being isolated spatially and culturally – us from the city, Perth from Australia and Australia from the world – arms one with an Atlas-strong sense of identity. Both actively and passively, originality seems to flourish in Perth's artistic community. Without the wider community's acceptance, creative pursuits lack the potential for commodification. There's no point in preening yourself for success because it's just not real. It's a fairytale.
>
> (Allbrook 2015)

Allbrook argues Perth would produce 'far less original art' were it a place where musical success was a common occurrence, laid out as some highly visible template: 'gigs to be got, managers to be found, reviews to be had and the ultimate dream of "making it" tangibly within reach' (Allbrook 2015).

Debunking myths about Perth

In focusing on how Perth's idiosyncrasies shaped his, Parker's and their friend's sound and scene, Allbrook perpetuates the twin myths of Perth's isolation and its 'boring' suburban nature. 'I used to dream about living in a cultural powerhouse like Paris or Berlin or New York,' he writes. 'But after spending time in these places I've realised that the emptiness and isolation of Perth – boredom to some – was a far better environment for creativity' (Allbrook 2015). He critiques Perth as an orthodox, banal, culturally isolated city where 'use of public space is regulated to the point of comedy, and Orwellian restrictions on tobacco, noise, bicycles, alcohol and public gatherings breed a festering discontent and boredom' (Allbrook 2015).

This aligns with decades-long perceptions of Perth being the 'most unrelentingly suburban of Australian cities' (Stratton 2008).[8] Just as the city's 1970s punk music 'took as its theme a rejection of Perth's suburban sprawl and the values and life-style that accompanied it' (Stratton and Trainer 2016: 40), Allbrook and his peers rejected their laid-back, suburban environment with 'music and art [which] have always been a way to manufacture that romance lacking in upper-middle-class Western Australia' (Allbrook 2015). He continues:

> This outlook was key to our musical and creative development. We railed against the boredom of Perth not with pickets or protest, but with a head-in-the-sand hubris that made us feel invincible and unique. We found more comrades along the way – Joe Ryan, Kevin Parker, Jay Watson – and together we erected great walls of noise and hair and mouldy dishes around our Daglish share house commune citadel on Troy Terrace where we incubated, practised, recorded, talked and grew.
>
> (Allbrook 2015)

In Perth, Allbrook argues, creativity isn't a commercial enterprise but an imperative, an irrepressible, imaginative impulse that cannot be suppressed and flourishes for its own sake in order to – paraphrasing Kurt Vonnegut, as Allbrook does – 'make your soul grow'. This philosophy 'helps to preserve a magical purity because it's executed with love – with necessity. And what's more, when [Perth] artists keep going and practising and advancing – which they must – somehow their crassness coagulates into something brilliantly individual and accomplished.' He concludes:

> Mundane and discouraging places like Perth create a vicious Darwinism for creatively inclined people, where survival of the fittest is played out with swift and unrepentant force

and the flippant or unpassionate are left behind, drowning in putrid mind-clag. You have to really need it, and without the mysterious and poetic benefits of a vibrant city culture this has to come from deep inside.

(Allbrook 2015)

This is no more true than of Kevin Parker, who 'grew his soul' jamming and gigging with friends while developing Tame Impala 'from deep inside', privately using his multi-track recorder to conjure music that was 'brilliantly individual and accomplished', to use Allbrook's words.

Interestingly, whereas Allbrook believed Perth's isolation and suburban nature fundamental to his creativity, Parker held different views. 'There's a big cultural cringe in Perth and it's cool [to say] Perth's so backward and, "Man, life in Berlin is so much more forward-thinking." But I kind of front the resistance to that,' Parker has said (Zammitt 2015). Similarly:

Lots of people make a big deal about Perth's isolation but I don't think it's really that significant, especially these days … I would be just as inspired to make music if I was living anywhere else.

(Lodown 2009)

Parker regularly gave interview responses like this in reaction to how music media would perpetuate myths about Perth, making them a key part of Tame Impala's narrative from the beginning. The first glowing international reviews of *InnerSpeaker* made a point of it, as much as calling out the album's vintage influences. *The Guardian* even uncharitably suggested it was due to Perth's relative isolation that 'no new music has reached it since 1969' (Hann 2010).

It's natural to think of music through the lens of where it hails from. Geography can (like genre) be a useful signifier.

As academics John Connell and Chris Gibson note, 'myths of place are often reinforced in music itself' (2003: 6), citing Frank Sinatra's and Billy Joel's odes to New York, and Public Enemy's and 2Pac's anthems about Los Angeles. Additionally, cities and regions with particular music production and cultural infrastructures can 'become linked with particular sounds, styles or musical approaches (such as the "Motown" sound, New Orleans jazz)'. Often, it's a combination of the two, a 'process of mythologising place in which unique, locally experienced social, economic and political circumstances are somehow "captured" within music' (2003: 14). We can easily add to this list: Seattle with grunge, Manchester with 'Madchester', Liverpool with 'Merseybeat'. But as Sarah Cohen points out in researching Liverpool's music scene, placing too much emphasis on associating cities with sounds and scenes risks creating 'reductive and stereotypical representation[s]' (2007: 53). As such, narratives linking a particular group or sound with place (again, like genre) tend to 'suit a strategic promotion of local authenticity by music and media corporations' (2007: 53).

In the case of Tame Impala, the psych-rock sound Parker pioneered alongside Allbrook and their peers became a huge influence, inspiring a wave of Australian acts from the late 2000s onwards (such as King Gizzard & The Lizard Wizard, Psychedelic Porn Crumpets, The Lazy Eyes, Death By Denim, Great Gable, The Babe Rainbow, to name a few). This earned Perth a reputation – like Seattle or Manchester in the 1990s – for being a hotbed with a singular style. This was another Perth stereotype Parker debunked, refuting the idea of a thriving local psych scene, instead pointing out it largely consisted of 'a circle of friends of maybe 10 or 15 people' that comprised an interconnected web of bands (Groves and Spring 2015).

Similarly, Jay Watson has elaborated there weren't many 'playing in this 2000s psych-rock scene ... it was more like a couple of share-houses. There were loads of other great bands we considered part of the scene but they were noise bands or garage rock or electronic guys we were all mates with' (Inscoe-Jones 2020).

Allbrook renders this exciting period vividly in *Creative Darwinism*, remembering a specific Amplifier Bar event as a:

> Microcosmic Woodstock – a tactile realisation of all the beauty and communion we cherished. The line-up included us (Mink Mussel Creek), CEASE (aforementioned stoner/doom/drone lords), Sex Panther (punk-party queens), Oki Oki (Nintendo synth pop) and Chris Cobilis (experimental laptop noise music) .... Nowhere else would such a ridiculously mismatched line-up consider themselves a tight community. We all partied together, played together and are still friends.
>
> (Allbrook 2015)

The uniqueness of Perth birthed this idiosyncratic DIY ecosystem and, in a second layer of anomaly, Tame Impala wound up becoming the most successful act to emerge from this very particular community.

These tangled, deep-set roots are crucial to Parker's artistic development. 'It was everything, it was all I knew ... I wouldn't be one-tenth of the musician I am today if it wasn't for those years and years of just playing all the time' (Brown 2020). Fundamentally, Tame Impala is Kevin Parker (with *Currents* marking the point he shed any impression it was a group effort), but his touring unit, long-time manager and support system comprise people from this late 2000s Perth community.

Rejecting (and embracing) Perth's influence

We've discussed how Parker was personally shaped by a close-knit local scene, but the extent to which the cultural experience of Perth permeates Tame Impala's music is more complicated. Parker has long maintained that geography has little influence on Tame Impala, instead placing greater importance on expressing his emotions and the sounds in his head. 'With *Lonerism*, we made half the album in Australia, half the album in Paris. In the end, for me music is such an internal thing, that to let the outside world influence would be against my modus operandi' (Groves and Spring 2015).

Unlike so many quintessential Perth bands over the decades, the city's unique location, culture and music history aren't explicit influences or characteristics in Parker's songs. There's no lyric that clearly expresses Perth's suburban experience, as the songs of Eskimo Joe or Bob Evans might, and earlier The Triffids and Dave Warner. He's never written a location-specific, politically charged anthem like John Butler Trio has ('Revolution'), or a song longing for home, like The Waifs ('London Still'). Nor has he ever used the metaphor of an endless, desolate highway to convey the distinctive WA experience of distance, loneliness and emotional dislocation following a break-up, the way David McComb did in The Triffids' Australian classic 'Wide Open Road'.

Tellingly though, loneliness and emotional turmoil are prominent, persistent themes in Kevin Parker's songwriting. Here we have a compelling evolution of the decades-long myth of Perth's isolation, Tame Impala expressing that notion not as geographical or spatial distance, but as a more deeply personal articulation of Parker's mental seclusion from the outside world. His social anxieties manifest in odes like 'Solitude Is Bliss' and an entire album titled *Lonerism,* with *Currents* then filtering those introspective themes through the lens of self-discovery, transformation and tortured romance.

Despite his global success, and downplaying Perth's influence, Parker often reflects on his upbringing as an important grounding force. He'd certainly valued the sun, sand and water of his hometown. He'd often 'go down south' – a common Perth phrase to describe a trip to WA's lusher South West region and popular destinations like Mandurah, Bunbury, Busselton and Margaret River. 'I just love being near the ocean … it's a luxury I've grown up with … It's a beautiful part of the world to get lost in' (Faulkner 2020).

That appreciation only grew as Parker spent more time overseas, discovering other places lacked the beachside lifestyle he'd taken for granted. '[It's] extremely rare, we discovered – I'm like, "Fuck, how do they live so far away from the beach? It's the most cleansing and spiritual thing in the world; how do they live without it?"' (Greenhaus 2015).

Parker has acknowledged how his teenage environment helped shape the sunny, spacious vibe of early Tame Impala. 'We'd drink, smoke weed and go to the beach. The music I was making was a soundtrack to what I was living' (Rogers 2015). The natural beauty of coastal WA also informed Tame Impala's debut album. *InnerSpeaker* was recorded at Wave House, a 50-acre property overlooking Injidup Beach with a 180-degree view of the Indian Ocean, about four hours' drive from Perth near Australia's South Western tip. Parker called it 'the most amazing scenery [he'd] ever woken up to' (Hockley-Smith 2011). Though, again, he de-emphasized its influence. 'I'm never one to say [the scenery] informed the music, but you know, it probably did a little bit! Because when you're staring at a beautiful ocean, anything you play is going to sound beautiful' (Gardner 2021). Parker must've had a sentimental attachment to Wave House; he returned to record drum ideas for *Currents* (Healy 2015) and in 2020, bought the property for $2.75 million (Newstead 2020b).

Additionally, Parker proudly splits his time living between Los Angeles (purchasing a US$4.2 million property in Los Feliz in 2019) and Fremantle, where he owns several properties (Macdonald 2025) and is the #1 ticket holder for the local Australian Football League (AFL) team, the Fremantle Dockers. He even composed a stomping, AC/DC-inspired theme song for the club (Fremantle Football Club 2021). Taken together, this smacks of more than rudimentary hometown pride. And Perth increasingly became a refuge for Parker from his celebrity status; a permanent reminder of his origins:

> Back in Perth, people don't treat me differently, I'm still just Kevin and no-one attaches any of this bizarre, constructed rock star status to me or any of the other guys. That's why Perth is a sanctuary. I can go home and be with my friends or disappear into the crowd like I used to.
>
> (Amies 2013).

Regardless of comments downplaying its significance on his music, I'd argue that Tame Impala is intrinsically linked to and influenced by Parker's environment. His 'Australian-ness' remains strong, particularly to international audiences, placing him in a lineage of globally recognized Australian music icons, from Nick Cave and Sia to 'our' Kylie Minogue, whose definitive Australian roots and identity remain despite their relatively fluid geographical and musical ties to 'Down Under'. Over time, Parker's attitude towards Perth's influence on his identity, and, by extension his art and creativity, appeared to soften:

> I used to say that I could be anywhere in the world, and I still like to believe that, because I don't believe that the quality or the style of the music that someone makes is dependent on where they are. However, there are many things that seep into your music and one of them is where you live.
>
> (Lawrie and Moodie 2018)

Where Parker lives, and spent much of his twenties, is Fremantle. Colloquially known as 'Freo', the historic port city experienced economic growth and media attention after hosting the 1987 America's Cup, following Australia's 1983 victory bankrolled by Alan Bond. Despite its gentrification, Fremantle has long been a thriving music and culture precinct since the 1970s, largely thought of as a bohemian 'alternative to conservative Australia', as local musician Abbe May put it (Lawrie and Moodie 2018).

Returning after living in Paris and completing *Lonerism*, Parker bought a ramshackle house near South Fremantle beach that he later converted into a studio, recording most of *Currents* there, and then also purchasing another home a few blocks away. A major source of inspiration while making the album was the South Fremantle Power Station, closed since 1985 and located on nearby Coogee Beach. '[It's] about 20 minutes walk away from my house, has been abandoned for around 30 years and allowed to slowly decay into this gigantic, derelict, empty, silent monolith,' Parker wrote in the liner notes accompanying the *Currents Collectors Edition*. (Parker 2017) He'd visit it 'numerous times', armed with headphones, notebook 'and just sit there next to it, usually to write lyrics but sometimes not even, I just liked being there' (Parker 2017). The location ended up inspiring not only the album's title, and an instrumental B-side[9] titled 'Powerlines', but served to reignite Parker's imagination when he was at a creative impasse:

> I couldn't believe how much the music opened up and spoke to me, made me feel all kinds of things again. A lot of the songs on *Currents* have passages that were directly inspired by the power house and doing laps of it. It is scary and confronting, but such a beautiful thing. I had one of the songs I was working on at the time on repeat and I wrote a lot of the lyrics down on South Beach. I suddenly remembered the value of being somewhere serene and beautiful and getting inspired in that way. I don't like to think of it as a necessity because music can be written for the purposes of escape. But so much of *Currents* was mentally conceived between here [Fremantle] and the power station all along the coast.
>
> (Lawrie and Moodie 2018)

This specific geographical inspiration for *Currents* speaks to the complexity of Perth's influence on Tame Impala. While Parker challenges the significance of the city's history, myths and character as central to his work, Perth remains crucial to his artistic journey. From the distinct milieu of the 2000s that enabled him to reach a worldwide audience via his bedroom, to the hyperlocal music community of friends he built, Parker's connection to Perth is evident. Ultimately, Tame Impala is both a product of Perth and a transcending of it, the story of how a creative individual can simultaneously push against and be shaped by their environment, resisting its importance but also, in subtle ways, embodying it.

3 B.C. (Before *Currents*)

In addition to the South Fremantle Power Station, *Currents'* creation was influenced by other key factors we'll explore: Parker's shifting views towards genre, a significant break-up and his work with British songwriter-producer Mark Ronson. But one of the most surprising catalysts came from a hometown prank.

At a wedding reception, Parker's friends arranged for the DJ to play a Tame Impala song, which cleared out the dance floor. 'It was such a rude awakening,' Parker recalled. 'It was awful! I was like, "Whaaaat? No-one wants to dance to Tame Impala?"' The incident made him 'wanna make music that people can dance to' (Smith 2020). Previously, Tame Impala was 'very much a kind of headphone, solitary experience, which is cool', Parker acknowledged, 'but I've moved on from that' (Britton 2015). His desire to make Tame Impala more danceable can be heard in 'Beverly Laurel', a *Lonerism*-era B-side featuring synths and Parker singing '*I know what's right for me*' on loop in the climax – a prototype for the techniques he'd perfect on 'Let It Happen' and *Currents*. Though rhythmically driven, the lo-fi production lacked the punch and polish of pop and dance music that Parker would later refine. In contrast to *Lonerism*, he envisioned making a 'silky ... high fidelity album' inspired by the 'clean, impactful sounds' of electronic, hip hop and R&B he admired. 'I started to idolize hip-hop producers and R&B producers more so than artists' (Hyden 2020).

Another *Currents* precursor was the side project Parker started with Tame Impala bassist Cam Avery, Ben Witt and Cam

Parkin. Between mid-2013 and early 2014, they performed psychedelic-funk-and-disco instrumentals at sporadic gigs under various absurd monikers: Cam, Cam, and Kevin's Groovy Groovy Funtime Disco Funk Elevator Explosion, AAA Aardvark Getdown Services, The Golden Triangle Municipal Funk Band and Kevin Spacey (Hanna 2014). In his 'Ask Me Anything' event with reddit fans, Parker said the project's 'whole idea was that it was a spontaneous performance that wouldn't have any "studio" or "recorded" version to go with it' (Parker 2015).

Jay Watson presciently described the music Parker made around this side project as 'disco, Michael Jackson megahits that he wouldn't use for Tame because he'd be too sheepish about it. But I'm trying to convince him to because they're all next-level *Thriller*-pop' (Harvey 2014). This included an early version of 'Daffodils', a track Parker later released with Mark Ronson for his 2015 album *Uptown Special*.

A passionate fan of Tame Impala's 'bedroom genius' (Rogers 2015) ever since *InnerSpeaker*, Ronson first met Parker in 2011 backstage at Australia's Future Music Festival. The pair quickly bonded over everything from 'ways to mic a drum kit to weird '60s songs', says Parker (Deville 2020). The two 'retrophiles and audiophiles' also shared a fascination for the way past music traditions could be used in modern contexts. 'We have old-fashioned tastes, but care about nothing more than making relevant music' (Deville 2020).

One particular conversation, in which Ronson and Parker imagined doing 'something cool' with funk after it had 'become this bad word' (Ronson 2021), led to Ronson inviting Parker to Memphis in late 2014 to work on *Uptown Special*, which featured the Bruno Mars-fronted mega-hit 'Uptown Funk'. Surrounded by session musicians and guest vocalists, the collaborative studio atmosphere made Parker think about his solitary creative process. 'It puts into perspective just how alone I am when I'm working' (Smith 2020). That rare autonomy was precisely what Ronson valued. 'He can play anything, and play it incredibly well. He has killer melodic instincts. And he has an impossibly cool aesthetic when it comes to sonics, without ever trying to be cool' (Cirisano 2020).

Parker played on several *Uptown Special* tracks, including taking lead on 'Summer Breaking', 'Leaving Los Feliz' and 'Daffodils', whose elements of yacht rock, lounge and funk were precursors to *Currents,* released six months after *Uptown Special.* 'Mark's a big reason why I had the confidence to do what I did with *Currents,*' Parker told *NME*. 'He showed me how pop music could have such a craft to it' (Smith 2020).

Kevin Parker: Studio wizard

By the mid-2000s, the divide between musicians and recording studio personnel (e.g. producer, engineer, mixer) was challenged and eroded by the prevalence of Digital Audio Workstations (DAWs) like ProTools, Logic and Ableton Live – Parker's software of choice. DAWs empowered what Adam Patrick Bell terms the 'musician-engineer hybrid' – creatives who not only play instruments and compose music but use the 'studio as a musical instrument' (Bell 2018), possessing the (usually self-taught) technical expertise to record, produce and mix music (Bell 2014). In this workflow, traditional stages like writing, recording and mixing merge into one fluid process, musician-engineers experimenting with software and listening to their results to evaluate their choices (Bell 2014).

Parker embodies this multidisciplinary approach, where his various roles are inseparable: 'I never know what's producing, mixing, songwriting – it means the same thing' (Savage 2016). The self-sufficient DAW paradigm empowered him to bypass professional studios with personnel, 'where there's some stranger telling you how to arrange your song [which] is pretty absurd', he reflected (Coyte 2015). For Parker, having multi-tracked and self-directed everything since age twelve, collaboration often means compromise. *Currents* is the visionary execution of this fiercely independent and idiosyncratic methodology; a singular artistic vision that simply could not have been made in any other way or by anyone else: 'All my greatest memories and musical discoveries have been made – just me, alone in a room, late at night … magical times. When I'm deep in the zone, it's like I'm in a room full of people, but it's all just me' (Danz 2023).

Parker says the initial discovery of 'a new bunch of chords, a melody, a few lyrics [is] by far' the most enjoyable part of the process. 'Generally, the first few hours that a song exists is the most magical [and] fulfilling' (Kingsmill 2012). Parker then becomes 'completely obsessed [with] throwing ideas down everywhere' and it's a drawn-out process reaching the finish line. 'The next two years are spent listening back to it, deciding whether I love it or hate it' (Kingsmill 2012). This creative approach engenders two key traits of Parker's compositional style. First, his gift for motifs – a leading phrase or figure that's repeated and developed through the course of a composition. The DAW allows Parker to flesh out his motifs, and on *Currents* he adopts an electronic producer's mindset, sampling and remixing his own material. Secondly, his exhaustive tinkering means his treatment – the way he manipulates hardware and software, engineers and processes instruments – is highly individual, forging dynamics, harmonics, textures and tones in uniquely personal ways.

The DAW's limitless potential is intoxicating but also potentially counterproductive. Parker spends countless hours tweaking instruments, or getting the ideal vocal. 'If I don't [nail it] in the first take, I'll do it on like the 500th,' he's said, even recording 1,057 vocal takes for one *Currents* track.[1]

This meticulous approach has earned Parker a reputation for perfectionism – a label he's uncomfortable with. 'I'm not on a quest for perfection,' he's said, calling his music 'rough and ready' filled with 'musical [and] mixing errors' (Konbini 2020). Instead, he describes his process as a 'cross between' perfectionism and spontaneity. 'I would hate to think my music is super controlled … because I love music that just comes out of nowhere. That is uncontrolled' (Newstead 2015). That tension between inspired, happy accidents and tireless refinement is central to Parker's creative philosophy:

> A lot of the things that actually end up on my albums – they're things that I just did straight in the moment anyway. It's just a spontaneous drum beat that I played, and then, because I'm such a perfectionist of how that moment happened, I have to preserve that moment, so I'm not allowed to go back and redo the drums, even though they're completely out of time, you know?
>
> (Newstead 2015)

Speaking of drums, on *Currents*, guitars play a supporting role to rhythm. Parker insists this wasn't a conscious decision: 'I never thought about how many guitars or synths there are on a song, it's like the furthest thing from my brain' (Konbini 2020). Instead, there's greater focus on Parker's first instrumental love: drums. 'Rhythms to me are almost more important than the music. It's the thing I spend the most time thinking about and imagining' (Newstead 2020c) more so than 'any other part'

(Deville 2020). And 'when you get a drum sound you nail, it's like ecstasy' (Konbini 2020).

American online music publication *Pitchfork* even called Parker 'the best and most underrated rock bassist of the 21st century' (Cohen 2015), further highlighting *Currents*' groove-forward instincts and production. Parker worked obsessively on the album, often from midday 'until 5 or 6 am' (Goble 2015; Kingsmill 2012). But listening was more important than 'actually recording', he explained: 'That's the crux of my process. It's 99% listening and then 1% do[ing] everything right at the end' (Newstead 2020c). In fact, he was still labouring over details the morning a taxi arrived to take him to the airport[2] for a flight to New York City to have *Currents* mastered. He continued tweaking lyrics and melodies mid-flight, then went straight into a studio after landing for more editing (Deville 2015; Newstead 2015). Originally due in January 2015, *Currents* was delayed to May, then July. 'I would never get anything done if I didn't have a deadline,' Parker admitted. Mixer Dave Fridmann once told him: 'No one ever finishes an album. You just run out of time,' advice Parker calls 'the quote of my life' (Newstead 2015).

4 'Yes I'm Changing': Track-by-track analysis

Track 1. 'Let It Happen'

We've already touched on it, but the revelatory importance of *Currents*' opener can't be overstated. Released nine weeks before the album, the nearly eight-minute 'Let It Happen' boldly exhibited Parker's eagerness to evolve artistically. Its crisp rhythms and prismatic synths grooved and glowed in ways Tame Impala never had before, owing more to 1990s electronica acts like Daft Punk and The Chemical Brothers. It felt like Tame Impala had moved from the Big Day Out main stage to the Boiler Room, to use an analogy fitting of that era.

The track even employs the EDM 'drop' technique, where a beat forcefully kicks in after rising tension. While not as explosive as a typical 2010s EDM drop, Parker's twist on the mechanic is nonetheless present and skilfully blends into Tame Impala's aesthetic to create something new. As critic Craig Mathieson noted, 'Let It Happen' 'sharpens the blissful drift that has been Parker's forte and gives it teasing tension and a lyrical defiance' (2015).

Though fusing psychedelic guitars with synths isn't new – The Beatles, The Monkees and The Doors added the Moog to their arsenal back in the late 1960s[1]– what's surprising is how Parker masterfully reinvents Tame Impala's signature sound, blending electronic music and prog-rock into a futuristic psych-disco hybrid – one without obvious contemporaries.

Partly conceived while riding Paris' Réseau Express Régional train system, the track conveys the locomotion of 'going through one landscape and into another', Parker explained. 'The rhythm rolls on. Sometimes you're in a tunnel, sometimes you're out in the mountains' (Konbini 2020). Lyrically, 'Let It Happen' preaches what its twisting, shape-shifting sound practises: surrendering internal struggles and embracing change, setting the stage for the album's themes of transformation and self-acceptance. As Parker told triple j host Zan Rowe:

> It's a powerful feeling when you realise that 'this is happening'. There are things that are changing, sometimes without your consent … It's quite a powerful thing, so much so that it felt like the whole album could be based around that feeling.
>
> (Newstead 2015)

'Let It Happen' is an outlier on *Currents*, few other tracks match its climactic energy, but also within Tame Impala's discography. Unlike the slower-burning intros of *InnerSpeaker* and *Lonerism*, it's a thrilling, immediate album opener, diving straight into an urgent pulse of gridlocked drums and stuttering synths beeping like an SOS.

Surging at a brisk 124 bpm (beats per minute), the track's trance-like repetition draws from another unlikely influence. Parker recalled:

> I was reading about Goa trance and these beach raves in South India and I remember thinking of the parallels to psych-rock. It wasn't about worshipping the artist onstage. The DJ was just a deliverer of the music. It would go on for hours.
>
> (Beta 2015)

Emerging in the 1990s, Goa trance describes communal experiences where ravers danced – often for days – to hypnotic techno. Parker saw psychedelic transcendence as the connection between this countercultural movement and the large-scale festivals Tame Impala inhabited by 2015, signalling his desire to make more communal music, and less guitar-driven nuggets for lonely music nerds.

'I've always loved listening to music on my own, but there's another side of me […] I wanted to make something [for] the club,' Parker said. 'I just realised that I'd never heard Tame Impala played somewhere [where] people were dancing' (Britton 2015). 'Let It Happen' makes sense on a dancefloor but substitutes EDM's typical feel-good platitudes and 'everybody dance!' sloganeering for spiritual self-interrogation. Parker renders personal transformation as simultaneously exhilarating and nerve-wracking, the intensity amplified through the track's corkscrewing momentum and shifting textures. This turbulence is highlighted by Parker's mildly overwhelmed vocals, with the titular refrain introduced early on and repeated as the music morphs and changes key. Structurally, the track toggles between two contrasting sections: a tense, looping A section that reflects the terrifying pull of the currents, and a more serene B section evoking zen-like acceptance, to let the tides take him where they may. This juxtaposition – of resistance and surrender – is captured through complex structure and unusual harmonic modulations.

The A section is loosely based in C# minor, implied by the insistent SOS synth playing C# repeatedly, though the chord progression never resolves to the root chord (I). Instead, it cycles through A (VI), F# minor (iv) and G# (V) with a suspended fourth interval that resolves briefly to a C natural. This sequence builds tension by avoiding resolution (to C# minor) and looping back to A (VI), left to '*all this running around*' – as the lyrics go – until the B section.

This style of tension and momentum draws from Daft Punk. Citing the 'god-like' French electronic duo's album *Discovery* as a major inspiration, Parker said, 'Let It Happen' was 'pretty Daft Punk-inspired' (Cirisano 2018), and you can hear how tracks like 'One More Time' and 'Digital Love' were touchstones, similarly building grooves on looping chord progressions and unresolved cadences.

Parker also runs his vocals through a keyboard sampler on 'Let It Happen' (starting from 5.29), giving them a robotic texture akin to Daft Punk's signature vocoder use. At 6.15, a metallic, heavily synthesized guitar riff enters, echoing *Discovery*'s guitar tones. The album's influence on *Currents* extends further. After pioneering the Parisian house music subgenre French Touch in the late 1990s, Daft Punk fused retro and modern sounds on *Discovery*, reaching fans across pop, electronic, hip hop and rock. Sound familiar? Identifying as a rock kid, 'Daft Punk weren't always something I actively listened to,' Parker told *Billboard*. 'They were part of a different world of music than I was … I know it sounds cheesy to say "it transcends genres" – but [Daft Punk] transcends worlds' (Lyons 2021).

At 0.56, 'Let It Happen' enters the B section, losing the SOS synth and modulating from C# minor to F# Major, an unusual shift in key signature smoothed out by a new chord progression: D# minor (vi), B Major (IV), C# Major (V), F# Major (I). This is an extremely common progression in pop music and provides the grounding harmonic resolution absent in the A section. Parker sings about hearing an alarm (at 1.20), namely the returning synth – now echoing a digital clock and returning us to the A section (1.27). After another full A and B cycle, the track settles into the A chord sequence before its climactic 'CD skipping' effect, the moment foreshadowed by a few hiccups before the groove glitches and gets stuck (3.50). Parker told

Rolling Stone he 'loved' the idea of listeners thinking 'the radio was broken or go, "Something's not right"' (Beta 2015).

It's the song's most memorable moment, suggesting the illusion of a DJ making an error before the omnipotent Parker reasserts control and reinstates an ecstatic groove. It also evokes the analogue quirks of physical media from a pre-digital streaming era. '[It's] about finding some way to alter your sense of what you're listening to … which way is up and down' (Beta 2015). Parker declared that disorientation is 'what psychedelia has always been about … All the stigmas and clichés aside, it's really just about transporting people, even for just an instant' (Beta 2015). He further argued psychedelia 'had nothing to do' with genre or processed guitars, it was a sensation, 'where you feel like you're outside your own skin' (Calvert 2015).

In this way, 'Let It Happen' and much of *Currents* use temporal dislocation to achieve the mind-altering listening experience of earlier Tame Impala albums but with a fresh twist. Where *InnerSpeaker* revitalized late 1960s and 1970s fuzz, and *Lonerism* expanded with richer textures, cross-breeding prog and pop instincts, *Currents* dives deeper. You hear 1990s house rubbing against sharp pop nous, 2000s hip hop and R&B production overlapping with 1970s soft rock. From song to song, even moment to moment, it's difficult to isolate what decade(s) Parker is channelling. And 'Let It Happen' is our first taste of this new normal, pivoting from Tame Impala's lysergic guitar-driven rock towards genre-blurring, era-hopping, unapologetically pleasurable songs.

After the bewildering 'CD skipping' glitch, low, synthetic strings (4.04) add a cinematic flair and a sense of embarking into the unknown. A snapping four-four, 'Billie Jean'-esque drum pattern and cyclical, ornamented synth build to another drop (5.05), returning to the A section and familiar lead melody. Where most songs would wind up around this point, 'Let It Happen' introduces new material, lifting off again, as if jettisoning booster rockets to push into orbit.

Parker's robotic vocals emerge, singing improvised 'gibberish' (5.34) originally meant merely as a placeholder. 'The first take [was just me] making sounds with my mouth … I didn't even know what I was saying,' he explained to *Under The Radar*. 'I do that a lot when I'm demoing and fleshing out ideas, because I've got the emotion in me, but I haven't turned it into words yet.' After several months, he tried recording real lyrics but couldn't recapture the feel he did when 'speaking in tongues'. Believing it fit the song's theme of surrendering control, he decided to leave it in the finished version. 'It will never make sense … but I guess fans will string words together and try to work out what I was subconsciously thinking' (Fink 2015b).

Live, Parker sings more formalized lyrics, but with slight variations between performances. As predicted, the fandom has offered their interpretations – converging into a loosely agreed-upon version:

> *Up at night thinking, you and I was dreamin'*
> *Try to get through it, try to bounce through it*
> *All the while thinking I might as well do it*
> *Baby that was so long ago and you know it*
> *Take the next ticket to take the next train*
> *Why would I do it and …*

At 6.15, the Daft Punk-inspired metallic guitar enters, with a sliding pattern that emphasizes the major 9th of each chord (e.g. B in the A Major chord), and repeats four times, with a slight ascending variation in the third. The gibberish returns (6.38), soon joined by a new, soaring counter-melody (7.03) where Parker sings about being ready to move on. Where the gibberish chanting suggests uncertainty, this soothing melody offers clarity and acceptance, a lyrical epiphany where fear gives way to growth.

The guitar motif reappears (7.14), uniting with the vocals towards a triumphant finish. The track grooves for another half-minute, gradually fading, symbolizing how personal change isn't finite. It's an ongoing process. Those themes are conveyed visually on *Currents*' cover art: a silver orb surging through rigid black-and-purple lines, leaving distorted ripples in its wake. Created by artist Robert Beatty from Parker's concept, this illustrated sense of change and momentum was inspired by vortex shedding, a fluid dynamics phenomenon Beatty interpreted as 'turbulent flow – basically the way a gas or liquid travels around an object' (Kesa 2015). We can interpret Parker as the orb, and 'Let It Happen' marks the start of his journey, coursing along the pink-hued path ahead on *Currents*.

Track 2. 'Nangs'

Following the odyssey of 'Let It Happen' is an unenviable task, but 'Nangs' excels at resetting our ears. At just 107 seconds, it functions more as an interstitial piece of sequencing, the first sign of Parker's thoughtful pacing on *Currents*, following the album's longest track with one of its shortest. 'I've always loved interlude sections, where it's not its own song, it's kind of like a connector,' he's said. 'Almost like an intermission in a film or something. It makes it more of a journey' (Zammitt 2015).

After the emergency-level intensity of 'Let It Happen', 'Nangs' eases us with its throbbing, oscillating synthesizer and warm drums reminiscent of the rhythmically dense, blown-out parts from *Lonerism* and *InnerSpeaker*. A wafting vocal repeats: *'Is there something more than that?'* over woozy keys and synthetic strings, vaguely echoing the self-scrutiny and 'CD skipping' effect of 'Let It Happen'. Like that track's gibberish, the ambiguously mixed vocals have fuelled fan interpretations, ranging from '*something wrong with love?*' to '*something wrong now*'. But the song's focus isn't so much on the words as the production.

As the title suggests, 'Nangs' also introduces the drug culture often linked to Tame Impala's music. In Australia, 'nangs' is slang for nitrous oxide (N_2O), a gas variously used for medical anaesthetic, boosting car engines and in whipped cream canisters (Australian Alcohol and Drug Foundation 2013). Its popularity as a recreational drug surged among young Australians in the 2010s, and as N_2O charges (also known as bulbs or 'whippits') became cheaper and more readily available, disused chrome canisters became a familiar sight at music festivals. A survey of 708 Australians showed an increase in nang use, from 25 per cent in 2013 to 54 per cent in 2020 (National Drug and Alcohol Research Centre 2023). Typically inhaled from a balloon, the gas produces a brief but intense high marked by euphoria but also dizziness and disorientation. The term 'nang' is believed to come from the distorted, repetitive sound some users hear during their high.

It's unlikely Parker was unaware of this association. 'Nangs' emulates that woozy sensation with phasing synths that gently pan from left to right speaker, gradually morphing from a buzz to an aqueous hum as the song progresses. The track begins with a reversed cymbal that resembles an inflating or inhalation sound. 'The first thing my friend said was "Man, you totally nailed the nang experience", Parker told *VICE*. "I did that only so it would sound cool. It's been a while since I've done nangs"' (Scott 2020).

Parker has never been shy about his drug use – including marijuana, magic mushrooms, LSD and ecstasy – or how they contribute to his creativity. He's described his recording process as 'like having a party by myself', indulging in weed, booze and food while working late into the night (Di Fabrizio 2020). A pivotal catalyst for *Currents* involved Parker, under the influence, having a transformative experience listening to the Bee Gees. He told *The Guardian*:

> I was in LA a few years ago and for some reason we'd taken mushrooms, it must have been the end of our tour. I was coked up as well, and a friend was driving us around LA in this old sedan. He was playing the Bee Gees and it had the most profound emotional effect. I'm getting butterflies just thinking about it. I was listening to 'Staying Alive', a song I've heard all my life. At that moment it had this really emotive, melancholy feel to it. The beat felt overwhelmingly strong and, at that moment, it sounded pretty psychedelic. It moved me, and that's what I always want out of psych music. I want it to transport me.
>
> (Perry 2015)

This anecdote bears much weight in *Currents*' mythos – not just for being vivid and memorable, but because it's a neat, if potentially reductive, encapsulation of the album's shift from psych-rock to a more soulful, disco-pop sound. It also echoes Parker's belief that psychedelia isn't confined to rock music.

As frequently as drugs are part of Parker's methodology and surface in fan appreciation, he regularly emphasizes he doesn't condone drug use. Per the same *Guardian* article with the Bee Gees anecdote:

> However, while he regards people choosing to listen to Tame Impala under the influence as the highest compliment, he doesn't take drugs to make music for people to take drugs to. 'I'd be disappointed if I was sat there with no ideas and

thought: 'Hey, maybe if I get stoned I'll have some ideas,'" he says. 'I'd feel quite defeated. At the same time, sometimes if I'm smoking a spliff halfway through a recording session it makes things sound more potent. When I had the idea for some of my best songs I was stone-cold sober. Some of my best songs I thought of stoned and recorded stoned. There's no correlation.'

(Perry 2015)

For Parker, weed and alcohol are tools for 'loosening up' in order to augment inspiration, but never to replace it. They amplify a signal – to follow a production metaphor – as Parker once put it: 'like turning up the volume of the ideas in your head. But you're just as likely to turn up a bad idea, as a good one, so I don't smoke if I want to think rationally' (GQ Australia 2015). He's also compared it to high-jumping athletics:

> If you can do it without drugs, that's good. If you can [jump] higher with drugs, that's great. But if you need drugs to get to that bar in the first place, that's not right. It should be in you regardless. People's imaginations and dreams are more fucked-up than drugs; it's just the sound of music in my head.
>
> (Iqbal 2012)

'Nangs' is a textbook example of how Parker's inspired production choices, made sober or otherwise, translate those potent internal sounds into something imaginative and immersive. The track's signature undulating synth has sparked much conjecture about its creation.

Numerous YouTube tutorials show fans recreating the 'wub wub wub' effect using the 'Greek Power' preset on a Roland Juno-106, a 1980s manufactured synthesizer (and a staple of Parker and his influences, like Daft Punk, Caribou and Mark Ronson). Others have achieved convincing recreations with a Roland JV-1080, a sample-based synthesizer module Parker acquired between *Lonerism* and *Currents* (Davie 2017).

This is just the tip of the online iceberg of gear-heads and budding bedroom producers dedicated to decoding the 'Tame Impala sound' – from Parker's dry, muscular drums to rich synth layers and processed vocals. You could go endlessly down rabbit holes unravelling his coveted techniques. But Parker downplays obsessing over high-end equipment. For him, it's about toying with sounds to render a resonant feeling, not chasing technical perfection.

'Nangs' is proof of that ideology. It doesn't need many words or a conventional runtime and structure to make a strong impression. A common fan reaction to the track is that it deserves to be longer, but therein lies its power. By leaving us wanting more, 'Nangs' gestures towards a larger sonic universe lurking beyond its 107-second duration. Like *Currents'* other brief-yet-impactful tracks, 'Gossip' and 'Disciples', 'Nangs' leaves space for listeners to imagine a fuller song while weaving into a grander musical tapestry. Despite its intermission length, it presents emotional and musical depths that echo across *Currents*. Only two tracks in, and the vast scope of Parker's vision is already coming into view.

Track 3. 'The Moment'

Following the hallucinogenic 'Nangs', 'The Moment' picks up where 'Let It Happen' left off, possessing similar themes of surrender through looping chords and lyrical anticipation. It also reinforces how Tame Impala's sound had evolved – moving from the glam-rock stomp of 'Elephant' and dreamy pop anthem 'Feels Like We Only Go Backwards' towards sleeker territory where keys, bass and drums play a greater role in driving rhythm and dynamics. Guitar takes a backseat, so when it surfaces for a solo (around 2.20) it lands with greater impact. Beginning with a snappy count-in, 'The Moment' is much closer to a strut than anything you can mosh to, and a big part of that is the song's drum pattern.

Driven by a shuffling 12/8 groove – a variation of 4/4 time signature that divides each beat into triplets – the rhythm accents the off-beat through syncopation, creating strong forward motion. This distinct pulse recalls Tears For Fears' 1985 hit 'Everybody Wants To Rule The World', and Michael Jackson's 'The Way You Make Me Feel' from *Bad* (1987), one of Parker's childhood favourites (Fox 2013). Mash-up videos of all three songs (with titles like 'The Moment to Rule the World' and 'Tame Impala Meets Tears For Fears) highlight their rhythmic similarities giving 'The Moment', along with its throwback synth sounds, a nostalgic flavour.

A slippery bassline complements the triplet feel of the drum groove, giving the track added bounce and energy even as the opening lyrics dwell in anxiety. '*In the end, it's stronger than I know how to be*,' Parker confesses, referring to forces of change outside his control, likening it to '*storm clouds closing in*'. The natural imagery recalls the overwhelming whirlwind from 'Let It Happen'. However, Parker's vocals are notably clearer and more present in the mix compared to past Tame Impala records, where he'd often 'bury' them in reverb, preferring a 'dreamy, silvery vocal sound' (Fink 2015b).

On *Currents*, Parker removes this sonic shroud, choosing to step outside his comfort zone and make his words easier to hear and therefore understand. 'It's something I've always wanted to do,' Parker explained to triple j's Zan Rowe. He'd always been confident in his lyrics but when it came to 'putting them out there, I kind of just recoiled in shyness'. With *Currents,* 'more than ever' he felt 'the music was the soundtrack to the message ... I knew if I didn't put the story out there, then I would regret it later' (Newstead 2015).

Parker's voice exposed and the emotional stakes rising, 'The Moment' expresses uncertainty about embracing impending changes, and how he'll feel when they inevitably arrive. *'I'll only know in the moment',* he sings in the first refrain as the music shifts towards the chorus. *'It's getting closer,'* he cautions, the 'ser' vowel echoing into an eddying vapour trail around the shifting chords.

A second vocal part emerges – *'I'm not ready ... I need a little more time'* – voicing internal anxieties in a layered reply to the lead vocal. First used in 'Let It Happen', this call-and-response technique becomes a recurring, prominent feature on *Currents* (especially in the closing song).

After the second verse and chorus, a kick drum mimics a racing heartbeat (around 2.05) before the groove relaxes into a sparse breakdown: growling bass synth, handclaps and sharp finger-snaps that are another recurring, unifying technique across *Currents*. A lonely guitar enters with a hooky melody and sleek, alien-sounding texture, created with a Roland GR-55 guitar synth pedal. This effects unit, also used in the climax of 'Let It Happen', also reappears throughout the album.

This section was 'directly inspired' by Parker's walks to the South Fremantle Power Station: 'There are parts of the song that when I listen to now I'm right back there ... Even the chorus, "*it's getting closer*", reminds me of the feeling of seeing it on the horizon and edging closer to it' (Parker 2017).

The guitar motif repeats as the shuffling groove returns, and in the second chorus, the anxious inner voice is joined by layered vocals now offering calm reassurance: *'Don't cry, we'll be okay ... breathe if you can'*. The mood lifts from turbulent to optimistic, embracing anticipation rather than dreading it. As Parker has explained, 'You've always tried to control who you are, control the world that you're in, but it comes to a point when it takes more energy to block it out than allow it to wash through you' (Calvert 2015).

That sentiment lands more clearly because Parker's vocals – previously cloaked in swirling, spacey textures – are now front and centre of a song about leaving things behind and embracing the new. As Parker reflected:

> A lot of my inspiration for lyrics has come from trying to deal with change, but also trying to deal with not having control. When you don't have to feel like you're in control of your life, it's daunting. When something is coming, and there's nothing you can do about it, it's scary. Making music that embodies that [feeling] is kind of like therapy. No one has control. That's the moral of the story.
>
> (Jenkins 2020)

These themes were evident on *Lonerism*, but where that album concerned 'being an introvert, separated from the rest of society', *Currents* is 'more about feeling yourself change as a person', says Parker; 'wanting to become part of the world, flourishing as a person' (Dapin 2015). Those realizations become even more explicit in the next track.

Track 4. 'Yes I'm Changing'

So far, *Currents* has explored change and acceptance, but mostly in abstract terms.

'Yes I'm Changing' is more personal, revealing an intimate trigger for Parker's existential self-assessment. A syrupy soft rock ballad built on soft-focus synths and crooning falsetto, the song depicts the demise of a relationship, Parker falling out of love as currents drift his life in a different direction. His confessional lyrics are backed by a simple four-four drum pattern, luminous keys and a gently insistent bassline.

The slower tempo (90bpm) and simple chord progression allow space to absorb the song's emotional core. Set in the common key of C Major, there's a focus on major 8th and sus2 chords – the inclusion of notes nine and two intervals from the root note, adding suspense and colour. The bass maintains rhythmic interest but hovers around the root (C) and third (E) notes, adding harmonic ambiguity to the verse's chord progression: C, CMajor9, Csus2 and CMajor7. A chordal shift to A minor (the relative minor of C Major) deepens the melancholy before resolving to the brighter C Major, where Parker reassures his ex not to be blue – there's a different future waiting for them, too.

Unlike earlier tracks, the tone here is calm and composed. The drums are minimal, focused on time-keeping with only a few fills (at 1:25, 2:08 and 2:41). And the fingersnaps make a comeback, augmenting the snare (most clearly around 2.45). Subtle, curated details abound, like the vibrant, arpeggiating harpsichord (2:53) ushering in a swell of distant traffic sounds (3.08), giving the already dreamy atmosphere a surreal twist. It's the album's most soothing track so far, a song of resignation laced with hope, crystallized in the tender concession: *'Yes I'm changing, yes, I'm gone / Yes I'm older, yes I'm moving on / And if you don't think it's a crime you can come along with me'*.

Compared to the 'poppiest' moments of Tame Impala's back catalogue, 'Yes I'm Changing' takes Parker into uncharted territory. Gorgeous melodies underscore emotionally direct lyrics, which along with the airy pads and crystalline chimes, recall the sound and subject matter of romantic songs from a bygone era. This nostalgic flavour heightens the yearning, bittersweet message concerning the end of one chapter birthing the start of another. The song would fit snugly on 1980s FM radio programming. Perhaps after 10cc's 'I'm Not In Love', Phil Collins' 'Another Day in Paradise' and The Cars' 'Drive'? Namely, the kind of soft rock acts once dismissed as inferior and schlocky by rock purists. But 'Yes I'm Changing' clearly signals Parker un-ironically embracing music he too once deemed a guilty pleasure. 'Yes I'm Changing' embodies how *Currents* embraces melody at its most ear-pleasingly direct. 'This time I challenged myself. I didn't obscure the melody,' Parker admitted. 'My old self would've seen it as too cheesy, too commercial, too top 40. The new me just sees it as what the melody wants to do' (Rogers 2015).

That melodic honesty is matched by lyrical candour, relying on simple rhyming schemes ('gone/on', 'see/me', 'do/blue/you') but also candid truths: '*They say people never change but that's bullshit. They do.*' Strikingly, Parker has no memory of recording the song initially:

> It was a weird experience, because it was [like] someone else made the song. I don't know where it was or when it was [made]. All I know is that I had this demo on my laptop and was listening to it going, 'This is really good. I wonder why I forgot about it?'

(Fink 2015b)

The song leans into simplicity, and finds power in sincerity, clear vocals and unembellished writing shifting focus to message as much as mood. 'Obviously, it's not like Bob Dylan', Parker reflected, '[but] it's a very lyrically-centered song … That's something that feels new to me, [songs] based on the lyrics […] "Listen to what I'm saying"' (Fink 2015b).

The verses parallel a romantic split with Parker breaking up from Tame Impala's old sound and from fans unwilling to follow *Currents*' sonic departure. Lyrics about change feeling inevitable, evolving into and embracing a new self, function as both apology and pre-emptive defence against impending criticism. Parker's self-reflexive lyrics acknowledge his decision to move on, both romantically and musically.

That departure becomes an invitation by the final verse: *'There is a world out there and it's calling my name / And it's calling yours, girl, it's calling yours too.'* The climactic refrain is sung over a comforting chord progression: CMaj7 (I) up to FMaj7 (IV) then Fminor6 (iv). It puts a positive spin on the ending, like a rom-com scene of two lovers parting, exploring separate paths to happy endings, the sun setting over the distant blaring of traffic. But real life is never so conveniently neat, and the next track confronts the hard, painful truths of ending a relationship.

Track 5. 'Eventually'

If 'Yes I'm Changing' is Parker rehearsing or imagining a peaceful resolution in his head, 'Eventually' concerns the painful reality of delivering heartbreaking news. After the idyllic strains of the previous track, the crackling static that opens 'Eventually' is dramatic, crashing into *Currents*' first big rock moment – guitar, synth and thunderous drums – recalling the swaggering 'Elephant'. But where that song was playful, 'Eventually' is deeply personal, with Parker facing up to the consequences of his transformation through tumultuous quiet-loud dynamics. Parker has said he enjoyed contrasting 'heavy guitar riffs' with 'really sensual … R&B melodies', likening the combination to 'The Flaming Lips meets Frank Ocean' (triple j 2015).

After the song's rocking opening chords, the verse is soft and sensitive, with warm organ, bass and delicate drums underpinning Parker's striking scene-setting. *'If only there could be another way to do this/'Cause it feels like murder to put your heart through this,'* he croons in a vulnerable upper vocal register. That interplay continues when the crashing rock motif re-enters (at 0.49) before the arrangement falls away again. A reverb-drenched fingersnap (1.07) leading to gentle keys backing Parker's devastating chorus: '*I know that I'll be happier, and I know you will too.*'

The chorus indicates that 'Eventually' shares the same key, C Major, and lush major 9 chords as 'Yes I'm Changing'. The chord progression descends – C Major (I), A minor (iii), G Major (V), and back to CMaj9 (I), with the sustained ninth note (D) adding a lingering unresolved tension before the sequence loops. However, when Parker sings the titular *'Eventually'* (1.35) it lands on a strong F Major chord (IV), the tonal emphasis accompanied by reversed cymbals and a flicker of distortion mirroring the song's opening. Additionally, Parker's *'ahhs'* are doubled by synthetic vocal harmonies that are equal parts heavenly and heartbreaking.

'Eventually' gives the impression of an electro-pop song with rock ornamentation, but also incorporates the dance music 'drop'. Transitions between phrases, like the rising harp (3.31) giving way to a lone snare hit, create dynamic tension and release. Despite its deceptively lean arrangement, 'Eventually' is full of these kinds of subtle variations. The synthetic strings joining the rock motif, for instance (2.21), or the second chorus adding synthetic brass and a high-pitched, see-sawing melody (3.13). These details don't crowd the mix, they enhance it. 'When you try and make something heavy, the less elements you have in it, the bigger it sounds,' Parker explained. Use too many instruments, and it muddies the impact (Davie 2017). Instead, he creates width and depth through layering, like doubling synth-organ lines and panning them hard left and right – a recurring trick in *Currents*' production.

The extended, carefully arranged coda (beginning 3.30) introduces more ear candy: a growling bass synth, rhythmic 'drops' of silence, more ethereal vocal harmonies and Parker freely jamming on drums (from 4.52). As he repeatedly sings '*eventually*', it becomes a single, hopeful mantra – a distillation of the old adage that time heals all wounds.

'The song is about knowing that you're about to damage someone,' Parker explained; 'almost irreparably, and the only consolation you get is this distant hope that they'll be alright eventually' (Fink 2015b). But it's more than just a break-up song. Parker wanted to bring a less common point of view – the perspective of the person who wants out rather than the one being left behind:

> I find there's a lot of poetry, art and songs singing about the plight of someone with someone changing in front of them. It excited me to tell the story from the other side. Trying to explain that it's not a bad thing, it's just natural … They're not going to be the one experiencing the pain that's dealt. They're the one dealing it. Arguably, it's just as emotionally crippling knowing that you're gonna do that. It's just as heavy. It's just as torturous.
>
> (Perry 2015)

A window into Parker's mindset, 'Eventually' is arguably the album's emotional centre. A poignant admission that letting go can be the right thing to do but not always the easiest. With that emotional weight still hanging in the air, *Currents* shifts into another interlude – brief, wordless but no less essential.

Track 6. 'Gossip'

Running just 55 seconds, 'Gossip' is a heady instrumental built from two parts: a pulsating synth and noodling, bone-dry guitar. The wavy synth was created using the Roland JV-1080's 'Flying Waltz' preset, used in a wealth of late 1990s R&B, house and techno music. (Reverb Machine 2018). It can be heard in Madonna's 'Nothing Really Matters'; P. Diddy's 'I Need a Girl Pt. 1'; Bone Thugs-N-Harmony's 1996 hit 'Tha Crossroads', and PlayStation video games *Tekken 2* and *Grandia*. The preset also featured in audio stings for TV's *Who Wants To Be A Millionaire?* and vintage Film Australia and MTV idents. Whether Parker chose it consciously or not, it's likely he was exposed to 'Flying Waltz' in his youth.

The synth's rhythmic pulse comes from a series of low-frequency oscillators (LFO) panned between speakers, giving it a ping-ponging motion. The other compelling ingredient is Parker's meandering guitar, recorded directly into his console (rather than a mic'd up amplifier) producing a dry, trebly tone and light buzz – a Tame Impala sonic signature.

If the wobbly synth and title of 'Nangs' evoked the sensation of a nitrous oxide high, the wavy synth of 'Gossip' suggests idle chatter. This interpretation is given weight by 'Flying Waltz' being constructed from four layered intervals of sampled vocal tones. Against this babble, the lone guitar could be read as Parker's inner voice – understated, resistant, offering differing melodic ideas against the hypnotic, eerie preset. The lack of concrete narrative, like 'Nangs', invites interpretation. Despite its brevity, and using just two components, 'Gossip' evokes much with so little. It serves as a palette cleanser that bridges the emotional 'Eventually' to what is to follow, and concludes the first of the two 12-inch records on the vinyl version of *Currents*.

5 'Eventually': *Currents* as 'break-off' album

Currents reflects Kevin Parker's personal life, particularly the end of his relationship with French musician Melody Prochet, whom he'd met while living in Paris and working on *Lonerism* (Spoto 2012). After living together in Perth and collaborating on her well-received 2012 debut album as Melody's Echo Chamber, they broke up in late 2013.

Sometime after, Parker reconnected with his high school sweetheart Sophie Lawrence. They dated, married in February 2019 and welcomed their first child, Peach, in early 2021. In February 2025, they announced a second child was on the way.

Many interpret *Currents* as navigating these two relationships; songs like 'Yes I'm Changing', 'Eventually' and 'Cause I'm A Man' are read as apologia addressed to Prochet, while 'The Less I Know The Better' and 'Past Life' nod towards Lawrence. Parker, however, resisted labelling *Currents* as a break-up album. As he told *Pitchfork*:

> It's more about this idea that you're being pulled into another place that's not better or worse … It's just different. And you can't control it. There are these currents within you.
>
> (Goble 2015)

Though he hasn't denied the autobiographical elements (it would be difficult to), Parker has devalued focus on his romantic life, preferring to accentuate broader themes of transformation, impermanence and self-realization. 'The break-offs in this album – I wouldn't even say break-ups because it's not meant to specifically be that – all those things are just part of this idea of feeling like you're moving on,' he explained. 'There's always this great lamenting about [things you leave behind], but that's just part of it' (Newstead 2015).

While *InnerSpeaker* and *Lonerism* were also autobiographical and explored change, *Currents* presents these themes more directly, its creator comfortable with sharing more of himself without obfuscation. 'Each step of the way of me making albums, I've kind of been breaking off more and more of myself,' Parker said. 'I discovered the fulfillment of really exposing myself and being vulnerable' (Zammitt 2015).

That vulnerability, Parker 'breaking off' himself in reflective and transformative songwriting, is on full display throughout *Currents*. Most notably, it powers the track that opens Side C of *Currents*' vinyl version, which transports us from the narrative 'present' (of the album's first half) to the past and Parker's youth, on what is the album's nostalgic centrepiece.

Track 7. 'The Less I Know The Better'

A mirrorball-lit tale of heartbreak, full of romantic intrigue and catharsis, 'The Less I Know The Better' is Tame Impala's most popular song by far, with more than 2 billion Spotify streams. The diabolically catchy falsetto and sticky rhymes make it irresistibly singable, while the space-age strut – a kaleidoscopic blend of disco-pop and glossy R&B – builds from an unexpected foundation: a bassline played on a guitar.

Specifically, a guitar pitch-shifted using a P-Bass preset on the Roland GR-55 unit, created in Parker's rush to record a demo capturing the chords and melody. The bass 'wasn't meant to be a focal part [and] the next day I listened back to it. I was like, "Oh, that bass guitar riff. That's got to stay"', Parker remembered (Fagerstrom 2022). It ended up being an invaluable part of 'The Less I Know The Better', hailed by Mark Ronson as 'one of the most iconic bass lines of the past 20 years' (APRA AMCOS 2021).

The take on the album is the first one Parker played 'within a few seconds of thinking of the song ... So, it's only about two bars of the riff, and it's just looped' (Fagerstrom 2022). The slippery bassline isn't the only illusion. As Parker revealed, 'every sound on the first two minutes of the song is the Roland GR-55', – the organ, strings, guitar, bass 'is all just guitar synth' (Fagerstrom 2022).

What makes the octave-hopping bass so smooth and satisfying is its use of major and minor thirds to outline the song's harmony, set in the key of E Major. The verses actually begin on the relative minor, C# (vi), then move through B/D# (an inversion of the V chord with the bass playing the third instead of the root note) and resolves to the root chord of E Major (I). The bass ascends as Parker's falsetto descends, but each arrives at the same, satisfying harmonic destination. In the chorus ('*oh my love*'), the same vi and I chords are flipped – starting on E Major (I), moving to C# minor (vi), then surprising us with a new flavour: D Major 9 (VII).

The track opens with the iconic bassline and a steady 4/4 drum groove (at 117 bpm). At 0.10, the mix blossoms, switching from low to high fidelity (a trick we'll explore in the next track, 'Disciples'). A looping three-note motif, played by guitar and synth, moves through changing chords that are filled out by glassy keys and a quiet, scratchy disco guitar part. Parker's vocal enters (0.25), mixed alongside the groove rather than in front of it through the verse. Another 'drop' transition pulls everything back but Parker's spacey harmonies, and a brief slide down the bass neck, bring us to the chorus (1.05) and its slimmed-down arrangement of vocals, bass, organ, drums and signature fingersnaps. At 1.39, two thuds of the kick drum turn us back to the verse. The end of the second verse, however, has a more distinct EDM 'drop'. Parker repeats his vocal line, and on the third repetition, the snare strikes every beat (from 2.15), subtly echoing the 'skipping CD' effect of 'Let It Happen', before returning to the chorus.

This second chorus uses the same two-thud turnaround and a sample of the song's opening bass hook (2.36). But instead of another verse – as anticipated – we're taken to an unexpected outro. This final section introduces a new melody and chord sequence: E Major (I), G# minor (iii), C# minor (vi), A Major 6 (IV) – a warmer, more natural progression than the prior chorus's surprise D Major 9. The texture shifts, too, decorated with synth strings (2.38), synth-brass (3.09) and tinny, crystalline bells (3.13). The looping three-note motif returns, now transformed into a major key colour by the new chord sequence.

Parker has playfully described 'The Less I Know The Better' as 'dorky, white disco funk … I wouldn't call it cheesy, but it's not trying to be too cool' (Fink 2015b). As such, Parker felt it sounded too 'way out' to belong on a Tame Impala album. 'To me it sounded like the Bee Gees or something' (triple j 2018). Parker almost gave away what would become his biggest hit to someone he thought better suited to giving it the disco-pop treatment: Mark Ronson. It was pegged for his *Uptown Special* album, until Parker played it for his girlfriend, who made him reconsider. 'She said "You're an idiot! You shouldn't have given it to him"' (triple j 2018).

After a few days recording in Memphis with Ronson, Parker worked up the courage to ask for the track back, and Ronson's guilt prevailed. 'He was like, "Oh yeah, dude, I was going to say this song is yours. I feel like I've stolen your hard drive!'" (Faulkner 2020).

The song's appeal goes beyond its addictive sound – it's the universal story of heartbreak at its core. The first verse paints a familiar scene of teenage drama – you can picture a young Parker at a party, booze in hand, watching across the room as his crush departs with someone else:

'Someone said they left together / I ran out the door to get her
She was holding hands with Trevor / Not the greatest feeling ever'

It's an economical verse, conveying setting, story and disappointment through a predictable '-er' rhyming scheme. It resonates because so many of us have been there – crushing on someone who doesn't reciprocate our desires, feeling like the dullest point in a love triangle. That ache tangles with obsession and sadness in the chorus, where Parker pleads with his crush before saying goodbye.

The song's surreal music video (114 million YouTube views and counting) gives the narrative a darker edge. A high school drama of lust and jealousy, it depicts the narrator as a basketballer, his rival Trevor as a literal gorilla and his crush as a hyper-sexualized cheerleader. Despite the resentment bubbling beneath the lyrics, the music's romantic swell makes us sympathetic to the singer's melancholy. We're rooting for him to get the girl.

Interestingly, Parker's role has reversed from 'Yes I'm Changing' and 'Eventually'. Here, he's on the receiving end of heartbreak rather than instigating it. Still, there's hope of a reunion, hinted at in the second verse:

'She said, 'It's not now or never, / Wait ten years, we'll be together'
I said, 'Better late than never / Just don't make me wait forever".

Parker clings to the naïve chance that though he's lost the romantic battle, he could yet win the war. 'That's one of the things that goes through your head ... you start going "oh, maybe it'll work out in the long term"', Parker reasoned (triple j 2018). In this case, it did. It's all but confirmed that 'The Less I Know The Better' was inspired by Sophie Lawrence Parker.

And what of Trevor? 'It doesn't take a genius to realize that Trevor is just Trevor because it rhymes with "together", which just means that Trevor can be anyone,' Parker revealed (triple j 2018). Even so, the character would take on a life of his own (see Chapter 6).[1]

'The Less I Know The Better' is full of contrasts: melancholic yet euphoric, wilfully nostalgic but forward-facing, its synthesis of disco, funk, R&B and pop feels both timeless and refreshing. For Parker, the song's optimism was shaped by his troubled upbringing. 'A place I went to in my mind a lot when I was a kid was, "Well, this is fucked but you know what? It's all going to be sweet in the future,"' he explained. 'It's a classic dreamer kid mentality' (triple j 2018).

Beneath its glossy exterior and love triangle trappings, the song captures more serious truths: life rarely follows your plans, and sometimes circumstances force you to surrender to the currents, no matter the consequences.

Track 8. 'Past Life'

Narrative-wise, 'Past Life' toys with time, detailing a random encounter with the same teenage crush from 'The Less I Know The Better' but years after that song's events. For the real-life Parker, he's 'breaking off' another personal moment for us, or at least taking artistic license with a moment from his own past.

The track opens at a leisurely 148bpm, with a kitschy keyboard phrase that descends, ascends twice, then loops. Parker's spoken-word narration enters – pitch-shifted and uncanny, reminiscent of Radiohead's 'Fitter, Happier' or Air's 'Suicide Underground'. It can be jarring on first listen, and subsequently, makes 'Past Life' one of the album's most polarizing tracks among fans. The surreal narration is juxtaposed with a mundane setting: picking up a suit from the dry cleaners. '*Thursday, 12:30*', Parker says in his distinct Aussie twang. '*I've got a pretty solid routine these days. I don't know, it just works for me.*'

Getting into his car, he glimpses someone in the rearview mirror, which triggers a subwoofer thud (at 0.38), heightening the moment along with echoed delay affecting the ends of Parker's phrases. '*Memories flooded back, stopped me in my tracks. Who was that? It was my lover.*' Garbled, heavily distorted bass overwhelms the mix (0.46) simulating Parker's being overwhelmed by this encounter with '*a lover from a past life*' (while also echoing the distorted opening of 'Eventually'). Familiar fingersnaps cue the chorus where a cluster of Parker harmonies sing the titular chorus, with the pitch-shifted narrator interjecting with the call-and-response technique (first heard in 'Let It Happen'). These sonic callbacks tie 'Past Life', and the impact of revisiting past romance, to the album's larger themes of transformation and emotional fallout.

The chorus introduces a crisp, hip hop/R&B-leaning groove (0.53) underpinning a chord progression in the key of B♭Major. The growling bass synth outlines E♭Major7 (IV) and F Major (V), with D minor 7 (iii) thrown in as a variation. The mix is coated with flanger – an effect where two signals are duplicated and their timing modulated – creating a sweeping, airy shimmer similar to a jet flying overhead. As the gargling bass subsides, the narrator continues, then a drum groove enters (1.25) paired with a chiming synth, flanger now soaking the lead melody. Parker describes this past relationship as '*surreal, poetic but uncertain. Like a bizarre chick-flick with a confusing end*'. Like the dry-cleaning anecdote, the casual 'chick-flick' reference roots the increasingly psychedelic sound in relatable banality. This disorientation symbolizes how love (re)entering one's life can turn even ordinary moments into something cosmic.

The chorus returns, layering in another call-and-response – a falsetto counter-melody – and a flanger-drenched drum fill (2.00), leading to a bridge section where the narrator talks about trying to move past the encounter.

The main keyboard motif disappears, replaced by a wobbling synth and glistening ornamentation. The narrator describes moving on with his life, but the encounter has consumed him. He now sees his life as a banal slog but doesn't want to stir up this old flame. Then he sheepishly wonders if she still has the same phone number. Maybe she does, he wonders. You can practically hear his cheeky smirk.

In the final chorus, the narrator wonders what's the worst that could happen by reconnecting with this past lover. It's an innocuous line loaded with irony given the complex emotional turmoil of earlier *Currents* tracks. 'Let It Happen', 'The Moment', 'Yes I'm Changing' and 'Eventually' – each has ably illustrated the 'worst that could happen'. As the arrangement blooms, the final chorus layers in more elaborate drum fills, synth textures and additional lyrics in the falsetto counter-melody. The track indulges in this dreamy soundscape until a telephone rings and a woman answers 'Hello?', concluding the track.

It's Sophie Lawrence Parker. Her cameo confirms her as the lover from a past life, lending weight to autobiographical interpretations of *Currents*. Yet, her voice also complicates the album's timeline.

From a narrative perspective, the events of 'Past Life' *precede* the emotional fallout of 'Let It Happen', 'The Moment' and 'Eventually'. This implies the real-world Parker was potentially 'switching off' feelings for Sophie while still disentangling from Melody Prochet. But rather than giving this gossip-y reading more oxygen, what's more compelling is the temporal disorientation this creates. Just as *Currents* blurs genres to avoid anchoring itself in a single musical era, 'Past Life' blurs time – it's psychedelic production, uncanny narration, and fragmented chronology all destabilizing the album's linearity. The past, present and potential future collapsing into one emotionally charged moment.

Track 9. 'Disciples'

Built on sugary melodies and traditional rock set-up (guitars, bass, drums, keys), the upbeat 'Disciples' stands as one of *Currents*' most overtly 'pop' moments. Just shy of two minutes, fans often lament this summery slice of ear candy is (like 'Nangs') criminally short, fading out as Parker self-knowingly sings about having so much he wants to tell us.

Running at 127 bpm in the key of F Major, 'Disciples' has just four chords, divided into pairs of rising fourths: F (I) to B♭(IV), G minor (ii) to C (V). A bright electric guitar outlines these chords while a fluid bassline emphasizes the root notes, driving momentum alongside rudimentary drums, often punctuating turnarounds with a double-time snare.

Parker's upper register falsetto is equally simple yet alluring. The melody hovers around the same tonal centre but plays rhythmically with phrasing and punctuation. This interplay between parts gives the track its bounce, and unlike the unresolved tensions of previous tracks, 'Disciples' relies on a satisfying harmonic resolution that loops.

A fizzy, squelching synth comes bounding in (at 0.33), adding a cute, naïve character. Emphasizing quarter notes, it eventually ascends into the song's standout feature: A flick of the switch effect that transforms 'Disciples' from lo-fi to full audio fidelity. The pleasing click's vintage flavour – like an old tape deck or TV button – evokes nostalgia, with fans likening 'Disciples' to a TV theme or advertising jingle. Parker says the song is 'about Seventies AM radio', even sampling static from an unused AM frequency.

To create the effect, he filtered out everything above 6kHz – 'someone told me AM didn't have anything past [that]' – then used a multiband compressor:

> So it had that compressed, boxed-in sound. When you turn it off, the song suddenly opens up. I love switching between the two, because your ears adjust [to lo-fi] … And all of a sudden, [the full range] kicks in, it's like this sensory, pleasurable thing.
>
> (Davie 2017)

The trick is so effective that it's repeated (at 1:31), reverting 'Disciples' from hi-fi back to lo-fi before its ending. These transitions aren't arbitrary – the first occurs before the chorus, symbolizing the narrator's changing relationship to the person they're addressing. Where they could once share things they wouldn't tell anyone else, that intimacy has been lost – the shift in fidelity reflects a longing for that deeper connection.

This changed dynamic is further detailed in the next lines: *'Now it's like the world owes you / Walking around like everybody should know you,' I wanna be like we used to / But now you're worried whose audience will lose you.'* The production pivot from lo- to hi-fi underscores the narrator's realization, and marks the shift from past (Parker's nostalgic AM radio concept) to the present. That epiphany is reinforced in verse two, with lyrics about being able to perceive a change in the person based on who they surround themselves with.

Despite the song's jubilant tone, the lyrics ache for something meaningful lost to time and change. As twangy guitar licks trail each vocal phrase, the second verse ends with a bittersweet sucker punch before the final flick of the switch: '*I used to take the long way / Just so I could walk past your door / I used to wait outside / But I guess I won't anymore.*'

While it's tempting, even rational, to assume 'Disciples' is addressing a romantic partner – perhaps the follow-up conversation that played out after the phone was answered in 'Past Life', or even written from ex-girlfriend Prochet's perspective – there's another compelling interpretation. 'Disciples' aligns with *Currents*' broader themes of transformation and Parker's self-critique about Tame Impala's change in musical direction, a concept introduced in 'Yes I'm Changing' and played out further in closing track 'New Person, Same Old Mistakes'. Taking the song's title as a clue, 'Disciples' is a meta-commentary sung from the perspective of a disillusioned fan reacting to Parker's sonic evolution. This proverbial disciple wants Parker's music to '*be like it used to / But now you're worried whose audience will lose you.*'

The ambiguity between romantic relationship and devoted fan is a playful way for Parker to embody and anticipate allegations he'd 'sold out', abandoning psych-rock for 'poppier' sounds. As he told *NME* in 2020:

> I always knew that *Currents* was such a new kind of sound to me. I knew that I loved it, and I knew that I wanted to do that, but I knew a lot of Tame Impala fans were going to turn

their noses up. I needed a lot of counseling from my friends and my girlfriend at the time. It was the first time that I knew that I'd let people down, because there were people who wanted *Lonerism* 2.0 … But I got a kick out of the fact that I'd be shaking the snowglobe up. All artists get a kick out of that – it's fun to ruffle feathers. I always wanted that and I was enjoying doing it, but when it came to releasing it I just felt bad. I'm always doubting the stuff I make, but with *Currents* it was the most amount of doubt.

(Smith 2020)

This context gives 'Disciples' and its flick of the switch a greater significance, symbolizing not only a sonic shift, but Parker's own transition towards a new musical identity. Though it's one of the 'poppiest' moments on *Currents* – and out of all Tame Impala's discography – 'Disciples' maintains the album's central theme of transformation, whether through age, experience, shifting desires or musical tastes. Indeed, the next track further challenges fan expectations.

Track 10. ''Cause I'm A Man'

Initially, ''Cause I'm A Man' scans as a droll corruption of Tame Impala's usual, spacey, mid-tempo psychedelia. It's a sensual, R&B-soaked track that invites comparisons to ballads by Michael Jackson, Prince or Lionel Richie. And that's no mistake.

'Michael Jackson's one of my favorite artists of my whole life,' Parker has said. 'In fact, I think he is my favorite. It's one of the first things I fell in love with before I learned about genres and before I knew what was cool to like' (Hyden 2015). Though he 'shut him out' as a grunge-and-rock obsessed teen, Parker rediscovered his love of pop music between *Lonerism* and *Currents*:

> Especially '90s R&B. Even when I hated it categorically, because I was supposed to, I still secretly loved these TLC and Jennifer Lopez songs. They were guilty pleasures, but when I grew up, I realized there's no such thing as a guilty pleasure. Then the world of music opened up to me – it wasn't like I was staring down this tunnel vision.
>
> (Greenhaus 2015)

Over a year before *Currents*, Parker casually uploaded a cover of Michael Jackson's 'Stranger in Moscow' to Tame Impala's Soundcloud account, giving the underrated 1996 single a spacey makeover but retaining its melancholic melody and sombre tempo. Jackson's lyrical ode to isolation also dovetailed perfectly with Parker's songwriting style. Though never officially released, in retrospect, the cover feels like a warm-up for *Currents*, and is most pronounced on "Cause I'm A Man".

The track gives pop-R&B a psychedelic spin, with syrupy melodies, lysergic atmosphere and laid-back groove – the album's slowest at 73 bpm. It feels weightless, floating on lush Juno-106 synth pads, while a smooth, octave-hopping bassline and understated drums provide enough funk-infused bottom-end to keep things moving. The structure is conventional (verse, pre-chorus, chorus) with melodic and instrumental embellishments signalling transitions. Notably, a sliding, descending synth hook (first heard at 0.03 then throughout) that's doubled in the chorus by buzzy, stereo-panned guitars. The ever-present fingersnaps (first heard at 0.26) supply rhythmic texture, while twinkling chimes (likely a Roland JV-1080 patch) decorating the harmony are made more prominent in the pre-chorus and synth strings beef up the latter choruses.

Parker's quivering, sultry falsetto – a rarity in Tame Impala's catalogue – channels soulful 1970s and '80s love songs, such as those by Marvin Gaye, Stevie Wonder and Bee Gees. But instead of romantic platitudes, he parades flimsy excuses for the heartbreak he's caused. He shows flashes of regret ('*each fuck up ... makes you cry*') yet deflects with lines like '*saying sorry ain't as good as saying why / But it buys me a little more time*'. Rather than take responsibility, the chorus shrugs: "*Cause I'm A Man, woman / Don't always think before I do*". Delivered with smooth indifference, it's a non-apology that stings all the more due to the silky music.

With its seductive swagger, "Cause I'm A Man' is easily Tame Impala's sexiest song, but also one of its most misunderstood. Some listeners and critics labelled the song sexist, even chauvinistic. *The Observer* cited its 'borderline dickery' (Empire 2015); another reviewer was unimpressed with the song's intended satire of toxic masculinity, saying it perpetuated the 'classic "boys will be boys" routine' (Tiny Mix Tapes 2015).

Parker expected backlash if the song were to be misinterpreted: 'I understand how it can be perceived as sexist, almost misogynistic, [but] deep in my heart, I am not in any way sexist' (Deville 2015). Originally conceived as a cock rock parody in the vein of Aerosmith or Mötley Crüe, Parker abandoned that approach as 'too obvious' (3voor12 Radio 2015). Instead of a masculine boast, he layered tongue-in-cheek lyrics beneath sensual R&B: '[It's] about how weak men are ... how we make all these excuses but really we're just these odorous male members of the animal kingdom. We don't have any self-control and are pathetic, basically' (Fink 2015a).

Some missed Parker's point, but the irony is baked into the tongue-in-cheek flourishes: The honeyed falsetto, unctuous groove, the comically orgasmic '*Ahhs*' punctuating the choruses (starting 1.38) – it's all a touch too flagrant, too self-consciously kitsch. Despite its sensual execution, Parker is roleplaying, skewering romantic music and masculine stereotypes rather than sincerely justifying shitty behaviour. It's understandable the punchline didn't land for everyone, besides 'Elephant' skewering its egotistical jock subject through a subversive glam rock stomp, satire has never really been Tame Impala's calling card.

Some artists understood the irony. LA sibling trio Haim remixed "Cause I'm A Man' without gender-flipping the lyrics, and Australian artist Ali Barter performed it for triple j's weekly covers segment, Like A Version. She called the lyrics 'so good! I love singing about the human condition and men singing about being a man' (triple j 2016).

This resonates with how Parker ultimately viewed the song, where the context of 'man' is reframed as shorthand for 'human':

> I maintain that only on the surface is it about gender. It's really about being human and how we as humans are vulnerable to our own urges or whatever. If you take out the chorus reference to being a man, all the rest of the lyrics have nothing to do with gender. I suddenly realised that all the lyrics about being a bad person, basically, could quite as easily be a reference to being a human.
>
> (Zammitt 2015)

That broader meaning – human fallibility – emerges in the final chorus: '*I'm a human, woman … I'll never be as strong as you / I'm a human, human / A greater force I answer to.*' "Cause I'm A Man' adds a lighter, ironic edge to *Currents*' heavier themes of insecurity and self-reckoning.

Track 11. 'Reality In Motion'

Bright and effervescent, 'Reality In Motion' is often regarded as one of the album's most underrated moments. It's brimming with gorgeous harmonies, delightfully wonky synths and a fuzzy bass pushing everything forward. There's even some prominent guitars. The reverb-soaked sound of the instrument plugging in (at 0.32) signals the chorus, where strummed chords shadow the synth, while dreamy harmonies frame Parker's reverb-steeped lead vocal.

Chugging along at 115 bpm, the track is in A Mixolydian mode and, like other album tracks, has a looping chord structure but without the same harmonic tension. The verses pivot between A (I) and G (VII), anchoring a relatively static vocal that prioritizes rhythm over melody. But then, the harmony subtly shifts: E/G# (V in first inversion) leads to D (IV), with a rising melody respectively accenting the thirds in these chords – G# in V and F# in IV. The chorus largely follows the same pattern, but substitutes D (IV) for G/B (VII6), another inverted chord – yielding the new sequence of: A(I), G (VII), A(I), G(VII), G/B (VII6), A (I), E/G# (V6).

The one exception to the otherwise stable harmony is a curveball pre-chorus section that disrupts the second verse (at 1.13), a piano playing a new progression: AMaj7, G#m7/A, F#min7 and G#min7/A. This would suggest a new E Major key but it's made murky by the persistent grounding note of A (the root of the original A Mixolydian mode but IV in E Major). This ambiguity creates uncertainty as Parker sings reflectively about fate and apathy. Roaming guitar and bass emphasize inversions – thirds, sixth, sevenths – adding to this section's floating harmony before resolving back into the definitive key and main groove of Gmaj7 to A.

While 'Reality In Motion' adheres to *Currents'* glossy sonic evolution, it also feels like a natural successor to material from *Lonerism*. The song has some of *Currents'* flashiest drums, including an intricate, dry EQ-treated fill (at 3.00) – a technique all over *Lonerism*. Unlike the directness of other *Currents* tracks, the language here is vague, revisiting the lyrical uncertainty and impressionism of *Lonerism*, offering metaphors (e.g. swimming in the deep end) and sensations (shivers, exhaling) rather than concrete meaning.

Within *Currents'* wider arc, 'Reality In Motion' is likely about approaching a milestone – a new relationship, or finally embracing personal change. Either reading fits, especially if the track was written in the transitional period between *Lonerism* and *Currents*, or Parker's break-up with Prochet and reconnection with Lawrence.

The bridge (starting 1.56) pulls back the drums, leaving just synth and vocal as Parker admits: '*It made my heart run in circles and overflow / And I was closer than ever to letting go.*' At 2.13, the harmony shifts between F# (vi) and G (VII), gradually building anticipation as the drum groove re-enters before fuzzy guitars and counter-melodies hover (through 2.30). The music swells as Parker sings about feeling alive, the bridge climaxing with the aforementioned drum fill and a return to the chorus.

Towards the song's end, Parker sings: '*Soon as I remember, baby, I surrender/I just need to breathe out*'; a reminder to himself as much as the listener. He concludes '*all there's left to do ... '* But we're denied the clarity of exactly what action needs taking because the phrase loops, backed by spiralling synths and cascading drums – recalling the 'skipping CD' glitch of 'Let It Happen'. Static rises, overwhelming the mix and abruptly cutting Parker – and the song – off mid-phrase.

This suspended resolution enhances the song's ambiguity. It's unclear if Parker is addressing Prochet, Lawrence or someone else entirely, and the lyrical vagueness makes it difficult to pinpoint 'Reality In Motion' in the album's narrative timeline. Though sequenced late in the album, the lyric about decisions approaching implies its events occurred before the decisive break-offs in 'Yes I'm Changing' and 'Eventually'. But then, is that before or after 'Past Life' and 'Disciples'? The song's upbeat tone means the drama is more buried than, say 'Let It Happen', but the anxiety is there in lyrical nods to earthquakes, emotional confusion and growing doubt.

In the final chorus, Parker tellingly sings: *'Let's not think about it/Put your arms around me, I can sense you doubt me.'* He intuits this relationship is unstable but rather than confront any trouble in paradise, he chooses to ignore it. Denial lingers beneath the brightness. As Parker once put it: 'You put your fingers in your ears and you close your eyes to shut [the whirlwinds of life] out … but it comes to a point when it takes more energy to block it out than allow it to wash through you' (Cavert 2015). Any sense of stability or contentment 'Reality In Motion' possesses is quickly disrupted as the next track pulls Parker – and the listener – back into the storm.

Track 12. 'Love/Paranoia'

Currents' penultimate track abandons traditional verse-chorus form for a stream-of-consciousness structure, unfolding in three loose sections. This gives the emotionally candid song a different flavour than the album's more accessible moments. It does, however, share DNA with 'Eventually' through heavy use of the Roland JV-1080 and Juno-106 synths (Reverb Machine 2022), reinforcing its thematic link to a break-up.

As the title suggests, 'Love/Paranoia' explores conflicted feelings of affection and crippling suspicion through angsty lyrics, right down to quoting what sounds like an argument: '*Does it really fucking matter, babe?*' *NME*'s John Calvert aptly called it a 'kind of "Jealous Guy" lament'" with Parker struggling 'either with current relationship hang-ups or old Parisian wounds, but certainly his own flaws as a partner' (2015).

These mixed emotions are expressed through shifting structure and harmony. Running at 111 bpm in the key of F Major, the song opens with a sequence that avoids the root chord – A minor (iii), B♭(IV), C (V), back to B♭ – mirroring emotional instability. '*I may not be as honest as I oughta be*' Parker sings as bell-like chimes augment the opening synth chords (0.10). Drums enter around the lyric about an arrow striking (0.18) alongside fuzzy bass and sampled vocal harmonies (similar to those in 'Eventually'). The track briefly softens (0.27) only to hit with another round of harmonies and a chattering sixteenth-note rhythm (0.35).

The song transitions to the next section (0.44), where a new chord progression, beginning on the root note, resolves the tension and brings in more of his beloved 7th and 9th chords: FMaj7 (I), B♭Maj7 (IV), Am/F (iii inversion), B♭maj9 (IV), D minor (vi). The arrangement pares back to foreground the vulnerable vocal, with reverberated handclaps and fingersnaps punctuating the delicate rhythm section. The track swells, with melodic embellishments (from 1.00) and the sixteenth-note rhythm returns, echoing through Parker's vowel sounds (like the 'ure' of 'insecure' at 1.10).

Parker sings with deepening insecurity about feeling like he's dying inside as strummed guitar and quickened drums (1.27) intensify the pace. A new bassline enters (1.49) emphasizing the 9th of each chord while layered synths swirl around Parker's growing mistrust. He wonders if he's going to cross a line, seemingly on the verge of spying on his partner's phone messages – a moment of paranoid self-sabotage. '*If only I could read your mind*', he pleads.

'Love/Paranoia' has often been interpreted as a cautionary tale, how unresolved trust issues can distort perceptions and poison happiness – either one's own or someone else's. The track can be read as the earnest yin to the sardonic yang of ''Cause I'm A Man', exploring similar themes of human fallibility through precarious harmony, structure and unpredictable dynamics. At 2.06, the music relaxes again as Parker confesses forlornly:

And suddenly I'm the phony one / The only one with a problem
True love is bringing it out of me/ The worst in me …

These words hit hard for anyone who's faced the painful truth that love can reveal one's deepest insecurities. The would-be hero becomes the villain, reminiscent of the role reversals from 'Eventually' to 'Less I Know the Better'. This theatrical reading is encouraged by the final section (2.20), where synthetic strings and brass arrive with cinematic flair and evoke Parker's memories of better times: '*Do you remember the time we were by the ocean?*' Delayed guitar joins (2.28) as the faux symphony swells around the chord sequence: F (I), B♭(IV), A minor (iii), B♭(IV).

As the final chord (D minor) lingers, there's a final juicy detail – a sharp reversed cymbal that ends the song (3.02). This sound was foreshadowed deep in the mix earlier (0.43 and 1.43), subtly warning this relationship was doomed all along. It's a sobering end before the final track, which reclaims control through accepting change.

Track 13. 'New Person, Same Old Mistakes'

Currents concludes with a six-minute epic that bookends opener 'Let It Happen' in theme, scale and talented ambition. 'New Person, Same Old Mistakes' also ties together the album's various threads of transformation and conflict – with lovers, fans and Parker's past self. It's a resolution Parker described as 'the final battle between optimism and pessimism. A confrontation between the side of you that wants to progress and the side of you that wants to stay the same' (Calvert 2015).

The track orbits around a central motif: a six-note phrase played across a squelching synth and subterranean bass part. Far from being repetitive, this motif evolves through various contexts in a compositional style comparable to, of all people, Ludwig van Beethoven, who'd expand motifs through increased scope and extensive development, most famously in his groundbreaking 'Eroica' and 'Fate' symphonies.

Haunting vocal harmonies open the track before the main motif is introduced, set in C Phrygian mode: C | D♭ | C | B♭ | A♭ | B♭. A slight variation appears in the fourth turn of the phrase, briefly injecting the third interval (E♭ – bolded for emphasis): C | **E♭** D♭| C |B♭|A♭|B♭. Backed by egg shaker and funk drums leaning on sizzling, syncopated open hi-hat, the motif interacts with a nimble counter-melody on synth (at 0.15). This agile, arpeggiating part outlines F (IV) and G (V) chords, creating a rhythmic and harmonic tug-of-war that embodies the song's core duality.

Mirroring the main motiif's melody, Parker enters: '*I can just hear them now "How could you let us down?"*' calling back to the fan-critique relationship theme of earlier tracks. But here the blame is also internal. Parker sings about two sides of his personality that can't agree, establishing the idea of conflicting factions. 'When I say "you," it's someone battling themselves inside their brain,' Parker explained. 'It's like this final showdown between this side of you that is embracing change and there's a side of you that's resisting it' (Deville 2015).

These sides clash in the chorus where, after a signature fingersnap (1.23), Parker sings: *'Feel like a brand new person'*. He's quickly undercut by a second, lower voice pessimistically responding in the same melody as the main motif: *'But you'll make the same old mistakes.'* This back-and-forth continues – the upper voice's hopeful lines (*'Well, I don't care, I'm in love'*) met with cautionary negativity (*'Stop before it's too late'*). 'Person' and 'love' here has, like the two sides of this internal struggle, dual meaning: referring to a new romantic partner (e.g. Sophie Lawrence) and Parker's love for his emerging sonic identity, embracing both personal change and evolving musicality.

At 2.03, the second verse responds to criticism: *"'I know that you think it's fake/Maybe fake's what I like ... not thinkin" in black and white.'* The term 'fake' here should alert us to Parker's changing attitudes to genre, specifically mainstream pop – something rock purists, his young self included, historically rejected as disposable, inauthentic. But this binary, narrow-minded view rejects the more complex grey area, as Parker told *Pitchfork*:

> Your morals on things change. When you start out you have this very black-and-white idea that people who are playing down-to-earth music are the ones that are keeping it real, and the ones making music for the masses – those 'commercial pop sellouts' – are fake, so you pick a side. But the longer you're in [music], the more disappointed you get meeting people you had these high expectations of, and you realize it's nothing like that at all.
>
> (Goble 2015)

Rather than embodying dogmatic loyalty to any one scene or style, *Currents* has showcased Parker's newfound freedom in pursuing his desires. In 'New Person, Same Old Mistakes', this is conveyed by the phrase concluding each verse where Parker verbalizes going after his desires, accompanied by a mysterious, noodling guitar (at 1.04 and 2.28) that's treated like a sample.

After another chorus and the internal argument – with the voices of 'the angel [and] devil on your shoulder' (Savage 2016) respectively panned to the left and right speaker – the song shifts dramatically into a bridge (3.04). Recalling 'The Less I Know The Better' and 'Disciples', Parker reaches for his falsetto range and uses a similar 'AM radio' trick to plunge the mix into lo-fi. The arrangement is confined to a standard rock set-up – guitars, bass and drums – and a subtle flanger effect (around 3.20) before a stinging guitar arpeggio (3.30) pierces through the lo-fi haze. Significantly adding to the bridge's transformation is a key change, from C Phrygian to E♭ Phyrgian mode, and a new melody breaking free from the central six-note motif. Parker sings a new melody that steps up through B natural – a note outside the original C Phrygian scale – to D♭ and E♭, then downward (E♭|D♭| B natural |B♭). This melody and its underpinning chord sequence – E♭(I), G♭minor (iii), and F♭minor (ii) – smooths out this unexpected modulation, hitting at a key emotional peak that contributes significantly to making 'New Person, Same Old Mistakes' so memorable. At 4.02, the track undergoes another transformation. Reversed synth plays arpeggios in descending then ascending intervals, sounding like raindrops rewinding into a cloud. The reversed effect fades (4.12) revealing clean arpeggios as the central motif returns on bass (4.16). A fuzzed-out synth line mirrors the motif but steadily develops and ascends into its own bittersweet topline as the 'raindrops' fade (4.31).

A crisp fingersnap 'drop' (4.39) ushers in the final chorus, which contains several subtle changes to lyrics and music. Dappled synth squiggles (from 4.52) and a second synth-guitar part (at 5.05) add to the climax, darting around the vocals. Significantly, Parker's lead line is no longer countered with negativity. Instead, a new falsetto counter-melody replies. The negative voice has vanished and with it, the anxious burden of insecurity. The central motif now includes a two-bar turnaround emphasizing A♭ and B♭, nudging the song's key from C Phrygian towards A♭ Major. It's extremely subtle – both keys contain the same notes, and we never get the strong resolution of an obvious A♭ Major chord – but it's enough to ease the looping motif's tension as Parker drifts, as he sings it, in a new direction.

'New Person, Same Old Mistakes' evolves from conflicted to triumphant, ending *Currents* on an optimistic note. It's a poetic ending that elucidates the core themes of transformation, impermanence and self-examination running through *Currents*, resolving the album's arc through sonic and emotional duality. Instead of a definitive ending, the track slowly fades out, suggesting life as an ongoing process of transfiguration, a series of constant choices and changes into a 'new person'. And that growth comes from within, not from external validation or criticism.

This philosophy clearly stuck with Parker. Discussing Tame Impala's 2020 album *The Slow Rush* and its closing track, 'One More Hour', Parker described it as 'about being on the edge of starting a new chapter. Stepping out into the world a new person'. He could just as easily be describing *Currents*' curtain-closer: 'It's about thinking, "How am I going to do this? How can I move forward? How am I going to go on with the rest of my life?"' Parker's own answer was simple: 'Be yourself. Do the things you like to do' (Di Fabrizio 2020).

That open-hearted belief signals Parker's maturation, but *Currents* was the turning point. Ultimately, it's an album about transitions, not destinations. It journeys through break-offs, romantic reunions, existential angst, zen-like acceptance, recognizing both loss and liberation. From its boundary-defying sound to its complex emotions, *Currents* chronicles its creator's personal and artistic transformation.

6 A.C. (After *Currents*)

Actively blurring boundaries between genres, *Currents* is a decade-defining release that mirrored how technology and tastes reshaped the sound, consumption and reception of music in the 2010s. We'll explore these shifts through four key themes: Tame Impala's success on Spotify; with vinyl buyers; Kevin Parker's rise as an in-demand collaborator and his surging internet popularity.

Disciples: Kevin Parker's internet fame

Already well-known in Australia before *Currents*, Tame Impala became near-ubiquitous in the album's wake, commanding colossal streaming figures, sold-out shows and major festival appearances, and an elevated online presence.

'Kevin Parker is Jesus', or so his immense, obsessive internet following would have you believe, disciples dedicating themselves to spreading the gospel of Tame Impala. The comparisons are initially surface-level – courtesy of Parker's shoulder-length mane and beard – but punch the phrase into an internet search engine and you'll be greeted with countless photoshopped images of Parker as Christ, often coddling a newborn lamb or a Tame Impala record.

References to 'Psychedelic Jesus' have long been a regular in-joke on r/tameimpala. Founded on 30 October 2011, the fertile reddit community labels its more than 500,000 active members as 'Disciples', a knowing wink to the *Currents* track.

Fittingly, 'Disciples' made its debut on r/tameimpala during Parker's AMA session on the platform, serendipitously, given the AMA saw Parker asked: 'How does it feel to be Australia's answer to Jesus?', noting his musical 'disciples' included Pond, Gum, Shiny Joe Ryan, King Gizzard & The Lizard Wizard, among others. 'I hope you don't actually think that,' Parker replied humbly. 'Haha! Can you imagine if I just agreed with you? like "Oh yeah it feels pretty good, lot of responsibility though"'.

An *Esquire* profile, titled 'The New Testament of Tame Impala', riffed on the Jesus trend, beginning with 'an indisputable fact: Kevin Parker is not Jesus'. Later noting:

> Although if he was, it would explain all the Kevin Parker-as-Christ art his fans make, and why they self-identify as 'Disciples', and why they caption selfies taken with him as their 'lord and saviour'. It would also make sense of their fervour, which seems religious in its intensity, as though they're experiencing his music as something more than music, something transcendental.
>
> (Banham 2020)

Much like the 'Tame Impala is actually one guy' meme, the origins of 'Kevin Parker is Jesus' is difficult to pinpoint. But some of the earliest references pre-date *Currents* by two years. 'If Clapton is God,[1] Kevin Parker is Jesus,' @ChuckWilbury tweeted on 9 August, 2013. Other early visual examples can be found on Tumblr, including user JayWhatson posting an image of Parker himself cosplaying as a stereotypical Jesus, posing in a bathrobe and draped scarf with two fingers of blessing held aloft. The image was shared, or 'reblogged', more than 1,500 times. The trend intensified around *Currents*; fans began proudly displaying bootlegged 'Kevin Jesus Parker' shirts and homemade signs at Tame Impala shows. The phenomenon arguably peaked at the 2018 Splendour In The Grass festival, where 'Disciples' gathered around a framed image of Parker. Organized by Facebook meme page 'triple j memes for Tash Sultana loving teens', the event attracted over 1.2k RSVPs and made headlines with Australian pop culture websites like *Pedestrian.TV* and *Junkee*. A video montage from the event featured a tongue-in-cheek prayer: 'As in Perth, as in heaven, just like Kevin. Give us today our daily dose of psych rock. Forgive us our sins as we forgive Trevor, who sinned against us' (Koslowski 2018; Tan 2018).

Trevor, the antagonist of 'The Less I Know The Better', had become an internet-fuelled phenomenon in its own right, with fans flooding triple j's textline with 'Fuck Trevor' messages. A large handmade banner bearing the phrase appeared at the 2015 Splendour In The Grass when Tame Impala debuted the song live.

'It just went from there,' Parker reflected on the meme's origins in a 2016 interview. 'Now there's not a show that we play where someone doesn't have a "FUCK TREVOR" banner' (DIY 2016). Parker even embraced the trend, posing backstage with one such banner alongside his partner Sophie in a photo circulated online. By December 2015, the same handwritten slogan was being sold as a T-shirt via Tame Impala's Instagram, with Parker and Jay Watson modelling the merchandise.

That a passing lyrical reference snowballed into an inside joke, and official merch, speaks to the size and strength of Tame Impala's fanbase. Need further proof? 'The Less I Know The Better' was voted the #1 song of the 2010s in triple j's Hottest 100 of the Decade poll (14 March 2020), besting beloved hits by Australian acts like Gotye, Flume, Violent Soho, and international heavy-hitters like Arctic Monkeys, Kanye West and Lorde. Parker, who grew up listening to the Hottest

100, called topping the poll 'a dream come true', adding he had a 'hunch' the track might top the 2010s countdown, calling it 'the little song that could' and crediting it with transforming his career. 'Every now and then, I have little sort-of nightmares if I hadn't written "The Less I Know The Better" … That song, undoubtedly, has played a big part in reaching new audiences' (triple j 2020).

Indeed, four years after its release, the track went viral on TikTok, the video-sharing platform's massive Gen Z user base sending streams skyrocketing. It jumped from RIAA (Recording Industry Association of America) Gold status to double Platinum (equivalent to 2,000,000 'units') in 2019, later achieving 4x Platinum in the United States and 10x Platinum in Australia (equivalent to 700,000 units).

Tame Impala is no stranger to the Hottest 100, charting nineteen songs across ten separate years, with *Currents* performing especially well: four tracks in the 2015 countdown, including 'The Less I Know The Better' at #4 and 'Let It Happen' at #5. Of Parker's many accolades, he values the Hottest 100 most: 'More than anything else that other people talk about being a huge deal. You know, like headlining festivals or Grammys or whatever. [It's] the closest thing to my heart' (triple j 2020).

If the public planted their flag with 'The Less I Know The Better', critics sided with 'Let It Happen' as one of the greatest songs of the 2010s, ranked as such in lists from *NME* (at #35), *Pitchfork* (#47) and *Rolling Stone* (#77). *Currents* has enjoyed a similarly enduring prestige, ranked in more than forty year-end lists from music outlets in 2015 and inducted into 'Greatest Albums' lists of the 2010s from *NME* (#71), *Pitchfork* (#79), *Billboard* (#32), *Stereogum* (#53) and *Rolling Stone*'s lofty '250 Greatest Albums of the 21st Century so far' (#148), among others.

As *GQ* wrote in their unranked 'Best Albums of the 2010s': '*Currents* matters because of how it reflects listening habits in the Spotify era, and the path forward that it lights for rock music, drifting back and forth between styles, paying little mind to outdated notions of genre or instrumentation. Its success demonstrates just how far open-eared music can reach' (Riley 2019). The point being that the transformation identified in Parker's artistry echoed a similar musical revolution brought about by the impact of streaming services.

Tame Impala's success on Spotify

Digital music streaming services – such as Spotify, Apple Music, Tidal and YouTube Music – drastically altered our relationship to music, and in turn, moved the entire industry from a 'transaction-based' model to an on-demand 'access based' experience (Spotify 2025a). Spotify, launched in 2008 and entering the Australian market in 2012, dwarfed the competition; its paid subscribers growing from 8 million in 2010 to 263 million by 2024, accounting for 675 million monthly active users (Spotify 2025b). Fulfilling the promise of retaining financial control after digital piracy decimated music industry profits in the 2000s (Zentner 2006), Spotify and its ilk gave consumers unprecedented access to vast libraries, available anytime, anywhere, at a few convenient clicks and swipes. This set 'an extremely low threshold for choosing to listen to something new, given that there is no extra cost or time involved in doing so' (Maasø 2018). This enables, and encourages, users to be more musically adventurous than they might ever previously have been.

A 2018 study of over 5,000 music streaming users concluded Spotify led users to consume more music, significantly increasing exposure to a wider variety of genres, artists, tracks, albums and 'facilitates discovery of more highly valued music' (Datta, Knox, Bronnenber 2018). Besides making music discovery more accessible, further challenging what separates 'mainstream' and 'alternative', some argued Spotify's subscription model and low royalty rates devalued music. In the years surrounding *Currents*' release, a chorus of high-profile artists criticized Spotify for inadequately compensating musicians, including Thom Yorke, Taylor Swift, David Byrne and Joanna Newsom, who damned the platform as a 'cynical and musician-hating system' (Roberts 2015).[2] Spotify wasn't always good for musicians, but it was good for business, becoming the industry's biggest earner through the 2010s. Not all music thrived under the new normal brought about by streaming but *Currents* certainly did.

In 2015, the year *Currents* was released, the Australian music industry experienced its first growth since 2012, with sales of $333.8 million. More than half (62 per cent) of that figure came from digital sales ($207.6 million), driven by streaming doubling its revenue (ARIA 2016). Who should be the face of this success? Kevin Parker, whose press shot appeared atop ARIA's report, despite *Currents* not being 2015's best-selling Australian album, ranking #28 in ARIA's 100 best-selling albums chart that year.[3] However, Tame Impala's streaming popularity made Parker the report's ideal poster boy, especially to younger, streaming-savvy audiences.

On Spotify, Tame Impala consistently ranks among the platform's top 200 artists, and of its 10 billion combined streams, more than half (5.1 billion as of July 2025) come from *Currents* (Kworb 2025). The album's expansive sound and appeal helped increase the likelihood of Tame Impala being picked by Spotify's recommendation algorithms. Thus, Parker's music appears in playlists including (but not limited to) 'Indie Rock Hits', 'Dance Hits', 'Coastal Drive', 'My Life Is A Movie', 'Neo-Psychedelic Rock', 'Beach Party', 'Aussie BBQ', 'Beast Mode' – you get the idea. That's before counting the countless user-generated playlists, filled with Tame Impala sound-alikes, with variations on the title 'tame impala vibes', or even 'Psychedelia for when you've heard enough Tame Impala'.

This playlisting phenomenon – organizing music by mood, genre and everyday tasks – is central to Spotify and capitalizes on using music as background to some other activity, a form of 'secondary listening' standardized as streaming became integrated into smartphones and everyday use through the 2010s (Lüders 2021; Weber 2009).

Spotify relies heavily on algorithmic technologies to analyse data from playlists, employing it for future curation, recommendation and automation. Consequently, as academics Jeremy Wade Morris and Devon Power note, 'streaming services aim to articulate, understand and, in some cases, even shape listener sentiments'. Ironically, this creates a self-sustaining feedback loop where the 'impossibly subjective nature of playlists entitled "Unrequited Love" [and] "Life Sucks"' frequently re-package the same songs and artists popular elsewhere on the service (one person's "Life Sucks" song is another person's "Caffeine Rush")' (Morris and Powers 2015).

As Spotify grew more dominant in the 2010s, so too did the industry's dependency on streaming and playlisting practices, creating a self-fulfilling ecosystem: the more streams a song received, the more likely it would be added to Spotify-generated playlists, leading to even more streams. Consequently, artists and labels began tailoring their music to meet Spotify's algorithmic preferences. Critics labelled this development 'Spotify-core' (New York Times critic Jon Caramanica) or 'streambait', coined by journalist Liz Pelly, disparaging homogenized, data-appeasing music designed to be 'inoffensive and mood-specific-enough to prevent users from clicking away' (Pelly 2018).

Is Tame Impala streambait? Parker's music shares some of the 'chill-pop-sad-vibe' simplicity that Pelly associates with playlist-friendly, 'zone out' listening; a product of 'playlist logic requiring that one song flows seamlessly into the next, a formula that guarantees a greater number of passive streams. It's music without much risk – it won't make you change your mind' (Pelly 2018).

However, while Tame Impala profited from this phenomenon, labelling it streambait is unfair. *Currents* isn't a product of data-driven trends, it anticipated them. The key term in Pelly's critique is 'risk', and *Currents* is where Parker took risks, moving away from his signature psych-rock sound. He recognized that writing a 'catchy, sugary pop song' was the 'yin to the yang of psychedelic rock' (Cirisano 2020), and how the tides were turning on tired attitudes towards pop. 'I actually believe that it's all getting more inventive and also the line between what is mainstream and what is alternative is becoming more and more blurred, which for me is a good thing' (Savage 2016).

Currents benefitted from the blurring of genre boundaries and ease of access ushered in by streaming, but rather than exploiting Spotify's algorithms, the album reflects Parker's individual artistic sensibilities and open-eared attitude, one that was more widely adopted through the 2010s. The album wasn't just big with the streaming crowd, but it was also a hit with the kind of audiophiles who pour over artwork and liner notes.

The vinyl revival

If the convenience of streaming made music into a more disposable commodity, then the 2010s presented a counter-phenomenon: the remarkable resurgence of vinyl – a vintage physical format once believed extinct. Despite physical media sales plummeting through the 2010s, vinyl defied the trend. Record sales grew from $1 million in 2010 to a staggering $42 million in 2023, surpassing CD sales for the first time since the 1980s (ARIA 2023). Though physical sales were niche (just 9 per cent of the overall Australian market) vinyl, along with streaming, was heralded as the 'star performer' driving the industry's growth, to the tune of $676 million, by 2023 (ARIA 2024).

Currents was very much part of vinyl's renewed popularity. It has spent 224 non-consecutive weeks in the ARIA Vinyl Album Top 20 since the chart's launch in April 2019, just behind perennial best-sellers like Fleetwood Mac's *Rumours* (242 weeks), Queen's *Greatest Hits* and Nirvana's *Nevermind* (both 227 weeks).

The popularity of *Currents* on both vinyl and streaming underscores Tame Impala's appeal with a broad audience. According to a 2015 *Grantland* profile, 25 per cent of unit sales from *InnerSpeaker* and *Lonerism* came from vinyl, emphasizing how the music resonated with different age demographics:

> [To] younger listeners who experience music via their phones and sprawling music festivals, and to aging music fans who fetishize physical media and new bands that fit old molds. These same futurist/retro impulses are embedded in Parker's songs, which come out sounding like record-collector rock

> but are assembled by a solitary polymath who sees himself more as an electronic artist than as a Jack White-style classicist.
>
> (Hyden 2015)

It's worth noting there's an increasingly large audience of young people that value vinyl for a variety of reasons, including the desire for a tangible connection with music. But the point of Tame Impala's dual appeal stands, and was also discussed by critics Jon Parales and Jill Mapes in a *New York Times Popcast* episode. Parales noted Tame Impala attracts 'lonely music nerds', who obsess over details. 'And it turns out there's a lot of us. And they're all standing there at Coachella [festival], singing along with Kevin Parker singing about being all alone.' Mapes agreed, identifying two 'very different' listenerships: The committed 'record store geek [that] Parker wants to cultivate and is himself', and a casual 'songs for studying to' crowd that stream Tame Impala as ambient background music. She questioned how much each group contributes to Parker's popularity, concluding, 'the jury's out for me' (*The New York Times* 2020).

Tame Impala's success with diverse audiences – whether vinyl enthusiasts, those streaming while multitasking; casual, hardcore; young, old – reflects the omnivorous music habits fostered by streaming in the 2010s. And 'no artist captured how genres cross-pollinated throughout the 2010s better than Tame Impala', as Josh Terry of *Vice* wrote when naming Tame Impala his Artist of the Decade. 'In the age of streaming and the big-box festival bubble, Parker's discography seems factory-made for both a crowd of thousands and a chill night alone with a vibe-heavy playlist' (Terry 2019).

Currents became a decade-defining album not just because it's popular on Spotify and vinyl (it undoubtedly is), but because of how it thrived amid sweeping cultural and technological shifts. The album confidently adapted to those significant changes in much the same way the music navigates its multi-genre, multi-generational, multi-dimensional nature. *Currents* also became a Rosetta Stone for artists looking to straddle commercial appeal with critical, cultural, digital and personal relevance. And plenty of talented ears were listening and taking notes.

'New Person, Same Old Mistakes': Kevin Parker's collaborations and influence

Another consequence of *Currents'* critical and commercial success was how it transformed Parker into a sought-after collaborator. His sound and sensibilities gained wider attention and influential acceptance in the mainstream through an increasingly substantial list of credits as a songwriter and producer.

Parker already had a history of collaboration (largely with his friends in Mink Mussel Creek, Pond, Melody's Echo Chamber and The Flaming Lips) but making *Currents*, he felt it was 'a big ad for me as a producer' (Wilkinson 2020). Its stylistic diversity would 'open a lot of doors' (Wood 2016), enabling others to hear the possibilities in Parker's music, fulfilling a long-held 'secret fantasy … The idea of writing a song and then not having to be the face of it. To be the guy pulling the strings – it's something I've always wanted to do' (Wood 2016).

Plenty of A-listers, from a diverse range of genres, heard those possibilities and sought Parker's services: pop sensations The Weeknd and Gorillaz, soul legend Diana Ross, R&B/neo-soul singers Kali Uchis and Miguel, fellow Australians The

Avalanches, bass virtuoso Thundercat. Parker also remixed music for Mick Jagger, Daft Punk, Crowded House, 070 Shake, Confidence Man and Mini Mansions.

In addition, *Currents* inspired covers that transcended genres – from metal (Northlane's 'Let It Happen'), bluegrass (Chris Thile's 'Yes I'm Changing'), and folk (All Our Exes Live In Texas' 'Eventually'), to string quartets, chiptune and children's lullabies. Artists like Ali Barter, Meg Mac and Ngaiire covered *Currents* songs for triple j's Like A Version, helping make Tame Impala the most covered artist in the segment's history. Additionally, legendary children's entertainers The Wiggles covered 'Elephant', an unlikely crossover that later topped triple j's Hottest 100 of 2021. (For more on this historic, yet controversial, victory, see Newstead 2022.)

The most pivotal *Currents* cover came from Rihanna, who closed her 2016 album *Anti* with a version of 'New Person, Same Old Mistakes'. The move surprised critics, audiences and even Parker. His management had been secretly asked for the song's stems,[4] unsure if Rihanna planned to sample or remix the track, but Parker complied. A week later, *Anti* dropped, with a near-identical version of the song save the title, 'Same Ol' Mistakes'. 'I guess that means she thought it didn't need changing in any way,' Parker told *Billboard*. 'It also meant I got 100 percent of the publishing [royalties], so I was like, "Fuck yeah!"' (Cirisano 2018).[5]

Parker originally intended 'New Person, Same Old Mistakes' as an R&B number to give to a female artist, much like how he'd briefly given 'The Less I Know The Better' to Mark Ronson. Hearing Rihanna's version made him realize how context could reshape a song. 'You can take a song that was on a psychedelic rock album and put it on a Rihanna album. You can stand back and say, "Hey, it kind of fits." … That blows my mind' (Cirisano 2018).

Rihanna's cover was significant in introducing the mainstream to Tame Impala, who were 'still quite firmly rooted in the indie world at that point', said Jodie Regan: 'Kevin hadn't done a lot of huge work with a lot of the people he has now, and he was way less well known.' Initially, people assumed the song was Rihanna's. 'They had no idea that it was a Tame Impala song. Then people started finding out, and that really led people to discover Tame Impala, and people loved it' (Stassen 2020).

The cover, combined with *Currents*' impact, springboarded Parker's profile, increasing demand from pop, rap and electronic artists seeking out his sonic stylings. The album redefined Tame Impala's identity – no longer misunderstood as a psych-rock group but a versatile producer-composer who could work across genres.

The path to pop

'His influence is everywhere; I'm sure he's influenced me in some ways', says Mark Ronson, who helped shepherd Parker towards the mainstream. 'Kevin's switched up his style so many times that he kind of influences a whole lane of music each time he puts a record out' (Ronson 2021).

Parker credits Ronson as 'a big producer mentor', teaching him 'how to incorporate what I do with other artists' (Cirisano 2018) and, unknowingly, modelling how to be a 'people person' in music: '[He's] so warm and humble and down to earth, but can communicate with anyone. So if I'm working with an artist – whether it's being a producer or a songwriter – I basically pretend that I'm Mark Ronson' (McMillen 2020).

In 2016, Ronson and Parker collaborated with Lady Gaga on 'Perfect Illusion', the lead single from her album *Joanne*. Described by Parker as 'kind of high-tempo thrash pop-rock' (Deville 2020), the track's synths and drums share DNA with *Currents* (especially in the demo version Ronson dropped into a 2019 DJ set in Melbourne). Parker, who appeared in the music video drumming as Gaga embraces him, described the song evolving from 'career move' to 'one of those life-career-defining moments [and] something so personal and meaningful' (Newstead 2016).

Similarly, in July 2022, Dua Lipa recruited Parker to work on her album *Radical Optimism*. Lipa, who called *Currents* 'one of my favourite albums ever … It just completely changed my life' (triple j 2023), fleshed out a Parker demo into lead single, 'Houdini'. He subsequently helped create eight of the album's eleven tracks (alongside co-songwriters/co-producers Caroline Allin, Tobias Jesso Jr., and Danny L. Harle). *Radical Optimism* reached top 5 in over twenty countries, securing Lipa a headlining slot at Glastonbury festival, where Parker joined her for a duet of 'The Less I Know The Better'.

These career moves helped fulfil Parker's aspirations to 'be a Max Martin' (Cirisano 2020), the Swedish pop mogul he'd once called 'the Darth Vader of pop' (Janssen 2017) for his roles behind chart-topping hits for Britney Spears, Katy Perry, Taylor Swift, The Weeknd and many others. Yet, Parker's influence extended beyond the mainstream charts.

Tame Impala's influence on hip hop

Parker's grooves, signature drum punch and synth-laden production resonated with evolving hip hop sensibilities in the 2010s, influencing its dominance over rock as the most-consumed genre in the United States (McIntrye 2017). Tyler, the Creator was one of Tame Impala's earliest rap supporters, expressing his love for *Lonerism* before *Currents* influenced his later work. Pulitzer-winning artist Kendrick Lamar reworked 'Feels Like We Only Go Backwards' (as simply 'Backwards') for the 2014 sci-fi film *Divergent*. Others followed suit with $uicideboy$ (2016), Maxo Cream (2018) and Kid Cudi (2020) sampling *Currents* tracks. Kanye West used beats supplied by Parker on 'Violent Crimes' for 2018's *ye*, while A$AP Rocky flipped 'Why Won't You Make Up Your Mind?' for 2018 single 'Sundress', performing it live with Tame Impala at Coachella in 2019.

Parker also co-wrote and co-produced 'Skeletons' with Travis Scott, for his breakout 2018 album *Astroworld*, alongside a cast of musician-songwriters in L.A. over multiple loud, late-night sessions. 'The air was thick with blunt smoke,' Parker remembered. 'I've never heard music played that loud in my life [and] your eardrums rattle ... Even listening to "Skeletons" now, it feels weird to listen to it at moderate volumes' (Cirisano 2018). Parker joined Scott's band for the song's live debut on *Saturday Night Live*, playing bass alongside guitarist John Mayer.[6]

Collaborating with hip hop's most revered practitioners deepened Parker's creative freedom, amplifying *Currents*' genre-busting attitude in future work: 'That's one of the strengths of hip-hop: It can be an absolute collage of sounds and flavours and ideas. In no other genre of music can things from so many different worlds come together and sound great' (Cirisano 2018).

Parker applied that philosophy, and his experiences with multiple collaborators, into the long-awaited follow-up to

Currents. Released in February 2020, *The Slow Rush* defied easy categorization, freely blending sounds from decades' worth of musical eras into another extraordinarily detailed sonic opus that was 'dance music-, hip-hop- and R&B-friendly, but still had the instruments that I love to use and a lot more of them', reflected Parker (Faulkner 2020).

What *Currents* made possible

The Slow Rush was met with critical and commercial acclaim, including five ARIA Awards (Album of the Year, Best Group, Best Rock Album, Engineer of the Year and Producer of the Year) and Tame Impala's third Grammy nomination for Best Alternative Music Album (following *Lonerism* and *Currents*). Although he didn't win, Parker later secured his first Grammy for 'Neverender', his collaboration with French electronic duo Justice, taking out the 2025 Best Dance/Electronic Recording.

In 2024, Parker expanded his collaborative resume and celebrity status further through two surprising ventures. First, a fashion line with chic Parisian label A.P.C. ('It definitely wasn't on my bingo card for my career,' Parker reflected [D'Souza 2024].) Secondly, co-founding hardware company Telepathic Instruments to develop and release an 'advanced chord generating synthesiser' known as Orchid (Telepathic Instruments 2024).

May 2024 brought another surprise, when Parker sold the rights to his songwriting catalogue to Sony Music Publishing, including Tame Impala's discography and his credits for aforementioned clients Lady Gaga, Travis Scott, Rihanna, Dua Lipa et al. (Newstead 2024a). Details of how much Parker earned weren't disclosed, but the sale was estimated in the tens of millions, following a larger trend where artists sold catalogues for blockbuster sums. Everyone from Katy Perry (US$225 million) and Bob Dylan (between US$300 and 500 million) to Bruce Springsteen ($550 million) and Queen (in a US$1.27 billion deal involving Sony) had inked similar deals to sell their publishing rights or recording masters. (For more on this trend, read Newstead 2024b.)

7 A few final thoughts

Looking back at the lonely, introverted teen from Perth, nobody could've predicted Parker one day being at the centre of a multi million-dollar deal, or rubbing shoulders with music's A-listers. It serves to remind us of Parker's unlikely journey, solidifying his place as a rare industry anomaly. And it was *Currents* that made all this possible, a visionary work where its creator evolved his psych-rock signature to participate in dialogue with the spheres of pop, rap, electronic, rock and beyond.

Few individuals – let alone Australians – are capable of what Parker has accomplished, in the way he has, with the same degree of acclaim and consequence. All while preserving his distinct sonic identity, artistic integrity and sizable fandom. *Currents* was the crucial turning point, a seemingly effortless display of intention and craftsmanship that announced itself with a confidence and ambitious quality that simply couldn't be ignored.

'All I can hope is that I make music that impacts me,' the ever-modest Parker once said (Clique TV 2020). But in the wake of its tenth anniversary, *Currents*' importance eclipsed the Perth native's hope.

It's difficult to imagine another Australian album of the 2010s that had such profound impact – not just on its creator, personally and professionally, but on the wider sound and direction of popular music. *Currents*' ripple effect cemented Parker as a revered sonic architect; a bright star in a constellation of modern music trends.

It speaks to the romantic notion of the artist's ability to change the world, and to truly appreciate *Currents* is to appreciate Kevin Parker's personal arc. You hear his growth across four cohesive, deeply rewarding albums, Tame Impala serving – as it always has – as the entity through which Parker expresses creativity, emotion and a multitude of kaleidoscopic sounds. *Currents* remains his brightest prism, where you can most clearly witness those concepts sparkle in a million colours. The proverbial jewel in his crown, the kind of rare, stunning sonic gem few are capable of crafting, and precisely what makes him a national treasure.

Notes

Chapter 1

1 During one astronomy lecture, Parker saw a diagram of Orion's Nebula, which later inspired the artwork for Tame Impala's debut EP.

2 Goetze and Parker still work closely together. As journalist Andrew McMillen put it in 2020 'Parker trust[s] Goetze's ears more than just about any other pair on the planet besides his own'.

Chapter 2

1 Famously featured on the cover to The Triffids' 1986 album *Born Sandy Devotional*, though that 1961 aerial photograph would be unrecognisable to today's very much more populated and gentrified Mandurah.

2 Let's not forget that Parker's father was em-bedded in the mining industry.

3 The Triffids, 'Wide Open Road' appeared in 1989 (at #68), 1990 (at #49) and 1991 (#52). Ammonia charted in 1995 at #27 with 'Drugs', and 1997 at #43 with 'You're Not The Only One'.

4 Eskimo Joe's 'From The Sea' at #3, John Butler Trio's 'Something's Gotta Give' at #7, Little Birdy's 'Beautiful To Me' at #8. The trend of WA acts reaching the pointy end of the Hottest 100 continued into the 2010s - with Tame Impala,

Birds Of Tokyo, San Cisco and Methyl Ethel - and the 2020s, thanks to Spacey Jane, who amassed 16 Hottest 100 entries in just six years.

5 Incestuous is exactly how Kevin Parker and bandmate Cam Avery would describe Perth less than a decade later (Davis 2013, Kerwick 2017).

6 That sentiment is immortalised in Tame Impala's 2020 song 'Lost In Yesterday': *'When we were living in squalor, wasn't it heaven?/ Back when we used to get on it four out of seven* [days a week].'

7 The full essay is well worth seeking out, doing a better job capturing the 'inspiring, productive' mid-to-late 2000s Perth music community Allbrook and Parker were caught up in than a large amount of academic literature can.

8 Allbrook's take on Perth and suburbia is somewhat simplified. For a more complex understanding of the Perth experience of suburbia, read Jon Stratton's 'The Triffids: The Sense of a Place' in *Popular Music and Society*, vol 30, no 3, 2007, pp. 377–399.

9 Historically, B-side refers to the literal flip side of a vinyl single - the song that typically received less attention than the A-side. For CDs, digital and streaming f-ormats, B-side is basically shorthand for a bonus or non-album track.

Chapter 3

1 'I can't remember if it was "'Cause I'm A Man" or "The Less I Know The Better", Parker told triple j's Zan Rowe (Newstead 2015).

2 This anxiety is chronicled in the *Currents* B-side 'Taxi's Here', with the lyrics: *'There's so much left unclear/But it's time, taxi's here'.*

Chapter 4

1 First by The Doors and The Monkees, on their respective 1967 albums *Strange Days* and *Pisces, Aquarius, Capricorn & Jones Ltd.*, and by The Beatles on 1969's *Abbey Road*.

Chapter 5

1 The name and rhyming scheme are reminiscent of British singer-songwriter Ian Dury and his late 1970s songs 'Clever Trevor' and 'Billericay Dickie', suggesting there's a more playful tone to 'The Less I Know The Better' that could otherwise be missed.

Chapter 6

1 This phrase, referencing guitarist Eric Clapton, became popular in the late 1960s after it was first spray-painted on a wall in London, burnishing his cult 'guitar hero' status.

2 There's plenty of research into the controversies surrounding streaming services and their financial implications, including Marshall (2015), Sinnreich (2016) and Hesmondhalgh (2021).

3 *Currents* ranked behind Australians Sia, Vance Joy and Hilltop Hoods but ahead of international acts Adele, Drake and Arctic Monkeys. The album continued selling well, ranking #69 in ARIA's top 100 best-selling albums of 2016, improving on end-of-year rankings for *Lonerism* (#94 in 2012, #90 in 2013) and *InnerSpeaker* (#97 in 2010). ARIA was slow to adopt streaming data – only factoring it into singles charts in 2014 and albums in 2017 – which may explain the lower rankings for Tame Impala's earlier releases.

4 The individual, isolated audio tracks of each instrument and element that make up a recording.

5 In the same *Billboard* interview, Parker says he learned from Kendrick Lamar that Rihanna had heard the song after neo-soul singer SZA played it for her during a studio session. 'She was like, "You've gotta check out Tame Impala"'.

6 Mayer was a noted *Currents* fan. In a 2016 Instagram post, he called it the 'best record of the past two or three years … Melody Heaven'.

References

3voor12 Radio (July 2015) '3voor12 Song Stories: Tame Impala – "Cause I'm A Man"'. Available online: https://www.youtube.com/watch?v=XLkYEdvEUVU&ab_channel=3voor12Radio

Alcohol and Drug Foundation (2013) 'Nitrous Oxide – Uses, Impacts and Risks'. Available online: https://adf.org.au/insights/nitrous-oxide/

Allbrook, Nick (January 2015) 'Creative Darwinism' in Julianne Schultz and Anna Haebich (Eds.) *Griffith Review 47: Looking West*. Perth: Griffith University. Available online: https://griffithreview.com/articles/creative-darwinism/

Amies, Nick (January 2013) 'Tame Impala: We Need to Talk about Kevin', *Tales from Down the Front*. Available online: https://ligger.wordpress.com/2013/01/16/tame-impala-we-need-to-talk-about-kevin/

APRA AMCOS (28 April 2021) 'Mark Ronson Presents "Tame Impala's Kevin Parker Wins 2021 Songwriter of the Year"', *YouTube*. Available online: https://www.youtube.com/watch?v=MiYYSyah1BE&ab_channel=APRAAMCOS

Arditi, David (2018) 'Digital Subscriptions: The Unending Consumption of Music in the Digital Era' in *Popular Music & Society*, vol. 41, no. 3, pp. 302–18.

ARIA (2016) 'ARIA Releases 2015 Wholesale Figures'. Available online: https://www.aria.com.au/industry/news/aria-releases-2015-wholesale-figures

ARIA (2023) '2023 ARIA Yearly Statistics'. Available online: https://www.dropbox.com/scl/fo/4ijzb1i3ozav48fn4tb3t/AEsz8u89gHu3d-APwmenjs8?dl=0&e=1&preview=ARIAYearlyStatistics2023.pdf&rlkey=a52tf1lxja3xb2t8oaxube8dk

ARIA (2024) 'Streaming Drives Fifth Consecutive Year of Growth'. Available online: https://www.aria.com.au/industry/news/aria-releases-2015-wholesale-figures

Australian Institute of Health and Welfare (2020) 'National Drug Strategy Household Survey 2019' Canberra 2020. Available online: https://www.aihw.gov.au/getmedia/77dbea6e-f071-495c-b71e-3a632237269d/aihw-phe-270.pdf.aspx?inline=true

Ballico, Christina (2012) 'Perth Bands Were All the Rage, Man! Routes, Routines and Routes of Popular Music, Explored through the End of Fashion', *Edith Cowan University*. Available online: https://research-repository.griffith.edu.au/server/api/core/bitstreams/2f0fb263-8e77-5ad3-aec1-c92225f0a0ff/content

Ballico, Christina (2013) 'Bury Me Deep in Isolation: A Cultural Examination of a Peripheral Music Industry and Scene', *Edith Cowan University*. Available online: http://ro.ecu.edu.au/theses/682

Banham, Tom (6 February 2020) 'The New Testament of Tame Impala', *Esquire*. Available online: https://www.esquire.com/uk/culture/a30776359/tame-impala-interview-the-slow-rush/

Bell, Adam Patrick (2014) 'Trial-by-Fire: A Case Study of the Musician–Engineer Hybrid Role in the Home Studio', *Journal of Music*, vol. 7. 10.1386.

Bell, Adam Patrick (2018) *Dawn of the DAW: The Studio as Musical Instrument*. New York: Oxford University Press.

Beta, Andy (May 2015) 'Tame Impala's Mind Tricks: Kevin Parker on Sense-Altering "Currents"', *Rolling Stone*. Available online: https://www.rollingstone.com/music/music-news/tame-impalas-mind-tricks-kevin-parker-on-sense-altering-currents-61070/

Blanchard, Bethanie (May 2010) 'Interview with Tame Impala's Kevin Parker', *Farrago*. Available online: https://web.archive.org/web/20120324154804/http://union.unimelb.edu.au/farrago2010/arts-and-culture/interviewwithtameimpalaskevinparker

Brabazon, Tara (2005) *Liverpool of the South Seas: Perth and Its Popular Music*. Nedlands: UWA Press.

Britton, Luke Morgan (20 May 2015) 'Tame Impala on Club-Friendly New Album: "I Realised We'd Never Seen People Dancing to Our Music"', *NME*. Available online: https://www.nme.com/news/music/tame-impala-57-1216796

Broken Record podcast (April 2020) 'Tame Impala (Hosted by Rick Rubin)', *Pushkin*. Available online: https://www.pushkin.fm/podcasts/broken-record/tame-impala

Brown, Eric Renner (October 2020) 'Patience Is a Virtue: Tame Impala's Psychedelic Journey from Perth to Arenas', *Pollstar*. Available online: https://news.pollstar.com/2020/10/05/patience-is-a-virtue-tame-impalas-psychedelic-journey-from-perth-to-arenas-2/

Calvert, John (14 July 2015) 'Tame Impala Interview: Inside the Mind of a Psych-Pop Shaman', *NME*. Available online: https://www.nme.com/features/tame-impala-interview-inside-the-mind-of-a-psych-pop-shaman-358

Cirisano, Tatiana (August 2018) 'Tame Impala's Kevin Parker on Sessions with Travis Scott and Kanye West, Surviving Hollywood & the Unreleased Music He's Sitting One', *Billboard*. Available online: https://www.billboard.com/music/rock/

tame-impala-kevin-parker-collaborations-interview-kanye-west-travis-scott-8471027/

Cirisano, Tatiana (January 2020) 'Tame Impala's Kevin Parker on His Pop Ambitions: "I Want to Be a Max Martin"', *Billboard*. Available online: https://www.billboard.com/music/rock/tame-impala-kevin-parker-billboard-cover-story-interview-2020-8549566/

City of Subiaco (2023a) 'Walking Subiaco: Jolimont and Daglish', *City of Subiaco*. Available online: https://www.subiaco.wa.gov.au/subiacowebsite/media/media/Community%20Development/Self%20guided%20walks/Walking-Subiaco-Jolimont-and-Daglish.pdf\

City of Subiaco (2023b) 'Daglish Local Heritage Survey', City of Subiaco *YouTube*. Available online: https://www.youtube.com/watch?v=xzQz4KEAW9Y&ab_channel=CityofSubiaco

Clique TV (15 February 2020) 'Kevin Parker de Tame Impala: "J'ai toujours été la princesse de la pop" - Clique Talk', *Clique TV*. Available online: https://www.youtube.com/watch?v=7fPoemFVOd8&list=WL

Cohen, Ian (2015) 'Albums: *Currents* – Tame Impala', *Pitchfork*. Available online: https://pitchfork.com/reviews/albums/20578-currents/

Cohen, Sara (2007) *Decline, Renewal and the City in Popular Music Culture: Beyond the Beatles*. London: Ashgate.

Collins, Sarah-Jan (19 January 2015) 'Triple J's Birthday: 40 Ways the Radio Station Changed the Australian Music Landscape', *ABC News*. Available online: https://www.abc.net.au/news/2015-01-19/40-ways-triple-j-changed-the-australian-landscape/6021220

Connell, John and Gibson, Chris (2003) *Sound Tracks: Popular Music, Identity and Place*. London: Routledge.

Cooper, Leonie (13 August 2015) 'Tame Impala's Kevin Parker on the Soundtrack of His Life', *NME*. Available online: https://www.nme.com/blogs/nme-blogs/tame-impalas-kevin-parker-on-the-soundtrack-of-his-life-15968

Coyte, Matt (24 July 2015) 'Kevin Parker's Dream World', *Rolling Stone Australia*. Available online: https://au.rollingstone.com/music/music-news/kevin-parkers-dream-world-747/

D'Souza, Shaad (July 2024) '"I Was in Dua Lipa's Dream": Tame Impala's Kevin Parker on His Surprise Glastonbury Duet – and Launching a Fashion Line', *The Guardian*. Available online: https://www.theguardian.com/music/article/2024/jul/22/tame-impala-kevin-parker-dua-lipa-glastonbury-apc

Danz (26 April 2023) 'Interview with Tame Impala', *Synth History*. Available online: https://www.synthhistory.com/post/interview-with-tame-impala

Dapin, Mark (June 2015) 'Why Tame Impala Are out of This World', *Sydney Morning Herald*. Available online: https://www.smh.com.au/lifestyle/out-of-this-world-20150624-ghwchk.html

Datta, Hannes, Knox, George, and Bronnenberg, Bart J. (2018) 'Changing Their Tune: How Consumers' Adoption of Online Streaming Affects Music Consumption and Discovery' in *Marketing Science*, vol. 37, no. 1, pp. 5–21.

Davie, Mark (March 2017) 'Tame Impala's: Current Nostalgia', *AudioTechnology*. Available online: https://web.archive.org/web/20230211150903/https://www.audiotechnology.com/features/tame-impalas-current-nostalgia

Davis, Michelle (20 February 2013) 'Tame Impala's Kevin Parker on Overcoming Lonerism', *Flagpole*. Available online: https://

flagpole.com/music/music-features/2013/02/20/tame-impalas-kevin-parker-on-overcoming-lonerism/

Deville, Chris (July 2015) 'Yes I'm Changing: The Bold Metamorphosis of Tame Impala's Currents', *Stereogum*. Available online: https://www.stereogum.com/1812044/yes-im-changing-the-bold-metamorphosis-of-tame-impalas-currents/interviews/

Deville, Chris (July 2020) 'We've Got a File on You: Tame Impala', *Stereogum*. Available online: https://www.stereogum.com/2090005/tame-impala-kevin-parker-interview-rihanna-gaga-kanye-coronavirus/interviews/weve-got-a-file-on-you/

Di Fabrizio, James (February 2020) 'Space, Time, and Psychedelics with Tame Impala's Kevin Parker', *VICE*. Available online: https://www.vice.com/en/article/space-time-and-psychedelics-with-tame-impalas-kevin-parker/

DIY (November 2016) 'Tame Impala's Kevin Parker Talks Making a Meme of Trevor in "The Less I Know The Better"', *DIY*. Available online: https://diymag.com/news/tame-impala-kevin-parker-interview-trevor

Douris, Rina (March 2021) 'Tame Impala's Kevin Parker Discusses The "Unlistenable" Music He Made as a Teen', *NPR*. Available online: https://www.npr.org/2021/03/24/980843066/tame-impalas-kevin-parker-discusses-the-unlistenable-music-he-made-as-a-teen

Empire, Kitty (July 2015) 'Tame Impala: Currents Review – One of the Year's Great Heartbreak Records', *The Observer*. Available online: https://www.theguardian.com/music/2015/jul/19/tame-impala-currents-review-kevin-parker-hearbreak-album

Fagerstrom, Bruce (May 2022) 'Tame Impala's Kevin Parker: "I've Rediscovered the Joy of Trying Random Chord Shapes and

Seeing What Happens. That's How So Many Great Guitar Parts Were Written'", *Guitar World*. Available online: https://www.guitarworld.com/features/tame-impala-kevin-parker

Faulkner, Noelle (January 2020) 'Tame Impala's Kevin Parker Is Finally Ready to Embrace Fame', *GQ*. Available online: https://www.gq.com.au/culture/entertainment/tame-impalas-kevin-parker-is-finally-ready-to-embrace-fame/image-gallery/a5d45ef369c6900b32808a76fbd942a5

Fink, Matt (2012) 'Tame Impala, Pop Fetishist', *Under The Radar*, Issue #40, Winter (March/April).

Fink, Matt (2015a) 'Tame Impala: Perfect Sounds Forever' in Mark Redfern (Ed.) *Under The Radar: April 2015* #53. USA: Wendy Lynch Redfern and Mark Redfern. Available online: https://www.undertheradarmag.com/interviews/tame_impala/

Fink, Matt (2015b) 'Tame Impala – The *Under The Radar* Cover Story Bonus Q&A, The Ocean Inside', *Under The Radar*. Available online: https://www.undertheradarmag.com/interviews/tame_impala_cover_story_bonus_2015/

Fox, Killian (April 2013) 'Kevin Parker: Soundtrack of My Life', *The Guardian*. Available online: https://www.theguardian.com/music/2013/apr/28/kevin-parker-soundtrack-my-life

Fremantle Football Club (22 May 2021) 'Our New no.1 Ticket Holder … Kevin Parker of Tame Impala!', *Fremantle Dockers Official Website*. Available online: https://www.fremantlefc.com.au/news/942093/our-new-no1-ticket-holderkevin-parker-of-tame-impala

Gardner, Josh (9 April 2021) '"Guitar Was My Everything": Tame Impala's Kevin Parker on 10 Years of InnerSpeaker', *Guitar.com*. Available online: https://guitar.com/features/interviews/tame-impala-kevin-parker-10-years-innerspeaker/

Goble, Corban (July 2015) 'Cosmic Neurotic: The Heady Perfectionism of Tame Impala's Kevin Parker', *Pitchfork*. Available online: https://pitchfork.com/features/profile/9683-cosmic-neurotic-the-heady-perfectionism-of-tame-impalas-kevin-parker/

GQ Australia (August 2015) 'Tame Impala: "Smoking Weed Can Make Music More Potent"', *GQ*. Available online: https://web.archive.org/web/20211016014350/https://gq.com.au/entertainment/music/tame-impala-smoking-weed-can-make-music-more-potent/news-story/fce9df7170ceffe3466d64d0e8c8f234

Greenhaus, Mike (June 2015) 'Tame Impala's Eclectic Currents', *Relix*. Available online: https://relix.com/articles/detail/tame_impalas_eclectic_currents/

Gregory, Jenny (2003) *City of Light: A History of Perth since the 1950s*. Perth: City of Perth.

Groves, Nancy and Spring, Alexandra (July 2015) 'Tame Impala's Kevin Parker: There's No Aussie Psych Scene, We're Just 10 People', *The Guardian*. Available online: https://www.theguardian.com/music/2015/jul/27/tame-impala-kevin-parker-interview

Hann, Michael (20 August 2010) 'InnerSpeaker: Tame Impala – Review', *The Guardian*. Available online: https://www.theguardian.com/music/2010/aug/20/tame-impala-innerspeaker-cd-review

Hanna, Jay (February 2014) 'Tame Impala's Kevin Parker Fronts AAA Aardvark Getdown Services', *PerthNow*. Available online:https://www.perthnow.com.au/news/wa/tame-impalas-kevin-parker-fronts-aaa-aardvark-getdown-services-ng-799356df3adafb5c4f30c410305e5087

Harvey, Rae (February 2014) 'Pond Mixed and Matched', *The West Australian*. Available online: https://web.archive.org/web/20140305132427/http://au.news.yahoo.com/thewest/a/21584303/pond-mixed-and-matched/

Healy, Pat (14 July 2015) 'Tame Impala: Swimming with the Currents', *Paste*. Available online: https://www.pastemagazine.com/music/tame-impala/tame-impala-swimming-with-the-currents

Hesmondhalgh, David (2021) 'Is Music Streaming Bad for Musicians? Problems of Evidence and Argument', in *New Media & Society*, vol. 23, pp. 3593–615. DOI: 10.1177/1461444820953541

Hockley-Smith, Sam (27 June 2011) 'GEN F: Tame Impala', *The Fader*. Available online: https://www.thefader.com/2011/06/27/gen-f-tame-impala

Howe, Renate (1994) 'Inner Suburbs: From Slums to Gentrification', in L.C. Johnson (Ed.) *Suburban Dreaming: An Interdisciplinary Approach to Australian Cities*. Geelong: Deakin University Press, pp. 141–59.

Hyden, Steve (June 2015) 'Tame Impala Let It Happen', *Grantland*. Available online: https://grantland.com/features/tame-impala-currents/

Hyden, Steven (4 February 2020) 'Kevin Parker Reviews Every Tame Impala Album, Including The Upcoming The Slow Rush', *Uproxx*. Available online: https://uproxx.com/indie/tame-impala-interview-the-slow-rush-kevin-parker/

Inscoe-Jones, Liam (17 June 2020) 'Tame Impala's Jay Watson Talks Perth, Young Thug, and His Fifth Solo Album as GUM', *The Line of Best Fit*. Available online: https://www.thelineofbestfit.

com/features/interviews/jay-watson-talks-perth-young-thug-and-his-fifth-solo-album

Iqbal, Nosheen (October 2012) 'A Trip Inside the Head of Main Man Kevin Parker', *The Guardian*. Available online: https://www.theguardian.com/music/2012/oct/06/tame-impala-kevin-parker-lonerism

Janssen, Stephanie (February 2017) 'Kevin Parker / Tame Impala', *Agolde*. Available online: https://mag.agolde.com/2017/02/02/kevin-parker-tame-impala/

Jenkins, Craig (May 2020) 'Tame Impala Made the Perfect Summer Album. Then Summer Got Canceled. Kevin Parker on The Slow Rush and Loosening Up in Quarantine', *Vulture*. Available online: https://www.vulture.com/2020/05/tame-impala-kevin-parker-interview-the-slow-rush-quarantine.html

Jones, Allan (September 2015) 'Tame Impala's Kevin Parker: "I'm Just Happier on My Own"', *Uncut*. Available online: https://www.uncut.co.uk/features/tame-impalas-kevin-parker-im-just-happier-on-my-own-70573/

Kerwick, Sean (3 September 2017) 'An Avery Far from Home: Cameron Avery', *DIY*. Available online: https://diymag.com/interview/cameron-avery-solo-debut-tame-impala-interview-2017

Kesa, Ingrid (20 July 2015) '[Exclusive] Designer Robert Beatty on Tame Impala's 70s-Inspired Album Artwork', *Vice*. Available online: https://www.vice.com/en/article/exclusive-tame-impala-currents-album-artwork-robert-beatty/

Kingsmill, Richard (September 2012) 'Tame Impala Interview 2012', *triple j*.

Konbini (19 February 2020) 'Tame Impala - J'ai écrit "Let It Happen" dans le RER | Interview | Konbini', *Konbini* YouTube channel. Available online: https://www.youtube.com/watch?v=8caT3Vg5S4M&ab_channel=Konbini

Koslowski, Max (July 2018) 'Watch Tame Impala Fans Hilariously Worship Kevin Parker at Splendour in the Grass', *Junkee*. Available online: https://archive.junkee.com/tame-impala-kevin-parker/168574

Kworb (2025) 'Tame Impala Spotify Top Songs', *Kworb*. Available online: https://kworb.net/spotify/artists.html. Accessed 2 March 2025.

Lawrie, Bill and Moodie, Claire (2018) *Freo Groove: Musicians on Fremantle*. Crawley: University of Western Australia Publishing.

Levin, Darren (January 2018) 'The Story of Spinning Top in 8 Records', *Inwy.co*. Available online: https://web.archive.org/web/20191106214520/https://lnwy.co/read/the-story-of-spinning-top-in-8-records/

Lodown (16 January 2009) 'Tame Impala. Chasing the Antelopes', *Lodown Magazine*. Available online: https://web.archive.org/web/20111111213756/http://www.lodownmagazine.com/index.php?page=26&modaction=showItem&id=556#page1

Lohkamp, Jakob (2023) 'Emotional Alienation and Online Sociality', *Cognitive Science Student Journal*, vol. 10, pp. 1–8.

Lüders, Marika (2021) 'Ubiquitous Tunes, Virtuous Archiving and Catering for Algorithms: The Tethered Affairs of People and Music Streaming Services', *Information Communication and Society*, vol. 24, no. 15, pp. 1–17.

Lyons, Patrick (12 March 2021) '10 Ways That Daft Punk's "Discovery" Predicted Pop Music's Future, as Explained by Fellow Artists', *Billboard*. Available online: https://www.billboard.com/music/music-news/daft-punk-discovery-anniversary-changed-music-9539516/

Maasø, Arnt (2018) 'Music Streaming, Festivals, and the Eventization of Music' *Popular Music & Society*, vol. 45, no. 2, pp. 154–75.

Macdonald, Kim (23 January 2025) 'House That: Tame Impala Frontman Kevin Parker's Surprise Buy in the Historic West End', *The West Australian*. Available online: https://thewest.com.au/business/housing-market/house-that-tame-impala-frontman-kevin-parkers-surprise-buy-in-the-historic-west-end-c-17479587

Marshall, Lee (2015). '"Let's Keep Music Special. F—Spotify": On-Demand Streaming and the Controversy over Artist Royalties', *Creative Industries Journal*, vol. 8, pp. 1–13. DOI: 10.1080/17510694.2015.1096618.

Mathieson, Craig (2000) *The Sell-In: How the Music Business Seduced Alternative Rock*. Milton: Allen & Unwin.

Mathieson, Craig (May 2010) 'Kevin Parker Talks Tame Impala, Roping in Friends and "Alone" Music', *The Vine*. Available online: https://web.archive.org/web/20120930094318/http://www.thevine.com.au/music/interviews/kevin-parker-talks-tame-impala-roping-in-friends-and-alone-music/

Mathieson, Craig (14 December 2015) '2015 Song of the Year: Let It Happen by Tame Impala', *Sydney Morning Herald*. Available online: https://www.smh.com.au/entertainment/music/2015-song-of-the-year-let-it-happen-by-tame-impala-20151214-glmv17.html

McIntyre, Hugh (17 July 2017) 'Report: Hip-Hop/R&B Is the Dominant Genre in the U.S. for the First Time', *Forbes*. Available online: https://www.forbes.com/sites/hughmcintyre/2017/07/17/hip-hoprb-has-now-become-the-dominant-genre-in-the-u-s-for-the-first-time/#5204d6355383

McMillen, Andrew (January 2020) 'How Kevin Parker's Tame Impala Conquered the World', *Weekend Australian*. Available online: https://www.theaustralian.com.au/arts/music/tame-impala-on-a-wild-ride-to-success/news-story/9f24b9394775cdf6f427ccd6a5b48c73

Morris, Jeremy Wade and Powers, Devon (2015) 'Control, Curation and Musical Experience in Streaming Music Services', *Creative Industries Journal*, vol. 8, no. 2, pp. 106–22. https://doi.org/10.1080/17510694.2015.1090222

National Drug and Alcohol Research Centre (2023) 'Ecstasy and Related Drugs Reporting System 2023'. Available online: https://ndarc.med.unsw.edu.au/sites/default/files/ndarc/resources/National_EDRS_2023_Final%5B1%5D.pdf

The New York Times Popcast (8 March 2020) 'The Unrelenting Space Jams of Tame Impala' (Hosted by Jon Caramanica. Produced by Pedro Rosado). Available online: https://www.nytimes.com/2020/03/08/arts/music/popcast-tame-impala.html

Newstead, Al (July 2015) 'Kevin Parker Tells Us 11 Amazing Insights about Tame Impala's Currents', *triple j*. Available online: https://www.abc.net.au/triplej/news/tame-impala-currents-kevin-parker-11-amazing-insights-interview/11998664

Newstead, Al (September 2016) 'Kevin Parker on Lady Gaga: "One of Those Life/Career-Defining Moments"', *triple j*. Available online: https://www.abc.net.au/triplej/news/tame-impala-kevin-parker-on-working-with-lady-gaga/11972610

Newstead, Al (March 2020a) 'Why Tame Impala's "The Less I Know The Better" Won Hottest 100 of the Decade', *triple j*. Available online: https://www.abc.net.au/triplej/news/hottest-100-decade-tame-impala-win-triple-j-less-i-know-better/12056978

Newstead, Al (1 September 2020b) 'Kevin Parker Buys Iconic Studio Where Tame Impala Albums Were Recorded', *triple j*. Available online: https://www.abc.net.au/triplej/news/tame-impala-kevin-parker-buys-studio-home-wave-house-innerspeak/12616250

Newstead, Al (17 February 2020c) 'Time Impala: Kevin Parker Goes Back to the Musical Future on The Slow Rush', *triple j*. Available online: https://www.abc.net.au/triplej/news/tame-impala-the-slow-rush-feature-album-review-kevin-parker/11971810

Newstead, Al (22 January 2022) 'The Wiggles' Historic Hottest 100 Win: How Tame Impala and Like a Version Stampeded to #1', *triple j*. Available online: https://www.abc.net.au/triplej/news/the-wiggles-historic-hottest-100-win-tame-impala-like-a-version/13724886

Newstead, Al (May 2024a) 'Tame Impala's Kevin Parker Sells Entire Song Catalogue to Sony Music Publishing', *ABC News*. Available online: https://www.abc.net.au/news/2024-05-16/tame-impala-kevin-parker-sells-song-catalogue-sony-music/103854954

Newstead, Al (April 2024b) 'Kiss, Springsteen, Katy Perry: Why Music's Biggest Names Are Selling Their Catalogues', *ABC News*. Available online: https://www.abc.net.au/news/2024-04-12/bob-dylan-katy-perry-why-musicians-are-selling-their-catalogues/103696602

Noisevox (2010) 'Noisevox Face Time Tame Impala Interview 2010 (Part 1)' Norris, John (interviewer), Harman, Rubes (producer), *Noisevox.org*. Uploaded to YouTube via @annieorangetree: https://www.youtube.com/watch?v=JoMbsf77rrw&ab_channel=annieorangetree

O'Bryan, Aidan (Director) and Landers, Janelle (Producer) (2009) *Something in the Water* [Motion Picture]. Perth: WBMC.

Parker, Kevin (29 April 2015) 'I Am Kevin Parker from Tame Impala. Ask Me Anything!', *reddit.com*. Available online: https://www.reddit.com/r/IAmA/comments/34clpm/i_am_kevin_parker_from_tame_impala_ask_me_anything/

Parker, Kevin (November 2017) *'Currents Collector's Edition'* booklet. Universal Music Australia.

Pelly, Liz (11 December 2018) 'Streambait Pop', *The Baffler*. Available online: https://thebaffler.com/downstream/streambait-pop-pelly

Perry, Kevin E.G. (July 2015) 'Tame Impala's Kevin Parker, from Psych-rock Stoner to Disco Infiltrator', *The Guardian*. Available online: https://www.theguardian.com/music/2015/jul/04/tame-impala-psychedelic-disco

Phillips, Keri (13 April 2016) 'The Mining Boom That Changed Australia', *ABC News*. Available online: https://www.abc.net.au/listen/programs/rearvision/the-mining-boom-that-changed-australia/7319586

Reese, Nathan (10 October 2012) 'Tame Impala's Loner Notes', *Interview Magazine*. Available online: https://www.interviewmagazine.com/music/tame-impala-lonerism

Reverb Machine (April 2018) 'Tame Impala's Gossip Synth', *Reverb Machine*. Available online: https://reverbmachine.com/blog/tame-impala-gossip-synth/

Reverb Machine (October 2022) 'Tame Impala's Love/Paranoia Synth Sounds', *Reverb Machine*. Available online: https://reverbmachine.com/blog/tame-impala-love-paranoia-synth-sounds/

Riley, Christopher (30 December 2019) 'These Are the Best Albums of the Decade', *GQ*. Available online: https://www.gq.com.au/entertainment/music/these-are-the-abest-albums-of-the-decade/image-gallery/447969fa7670aed9ff9f347191aacbab

Roberts, Randall (18 October 2015) 'Q&A: Joanna Newsom Calls Spotify 'A Villainous Cabal' and 'A Garbage System', *Los Angeles Times*. Available online: https://www.latimes.com/entertainment/music/posts/la-et-ms-joanna-newsom-spotify-villainous-cabal-garbage-system-20151015-story.html

Rogers, Ray (July 2015) 'Tame Impala's Kevin Parker Is Ready to Jump from Reclusive Studio Whiz to Global Alt-Rock God', *Billboard*. Available online: https://www.billboard.com/music/rock/tame-impala-kevin-parker-interview-mark-ronson-6641772/

Ronson, Mark (23 March 2021) 'Tame for Heroes: Mark Ronson on the Legacy of Tame Impala's "Innerspeaker"', *DIY*. Available online: https://diymag.com/feature/mark-ronson-tame-impala-innerspeaker-march-2021

Savage, Jon (2016) 'The New Pop: Kevin Parker' in Max Pearmain (Ed.) *Arena Homme + 45: Summer/Autumn 2016*. London: Bauer Media.

Scott, Tim (2020) 'Please Don't Call Tame Impala's Kevin Parker a Perfectionist', VICE. Available online:https://www.vice.com/en/article/please-dont-call-call-tame-impalas-kevin-parker-a-perfectionist/

Sinnreich, Aram (2016) 'Slicing the Pie: The Search for an Equitable Recorded Music Economy' in Patrik Wikström and Robert DeFillippi (Eds.) *Business Innovation and Disruption in the Music Industry*. UK: Edward Elgar Publishing.

Smith, Mark (2015) 'That's How Insanity Happens: Kevin Parker (Tame Impala)' in A.J. Samuels and Mark Smith (Eds.) *Electronic Beats Magazine Issue 3/Fall 2015*. Berlin: Telekom Electronic Beats.

Smith, Thomas (14 July 2020) 'Tame Impala's Currents at Five: Kevin Parker Takes Us Inside the Breakthrough Disco-pop opus', *NME*. Available online: https://www.nme.com/features/tame-impala-currents-fifth-anniversary-interview-2020-rihanna-2706819

Spotify (2025a) 'About Spotify'. Available online: https://investors.spotify.com/about/. Accessed 28 February 2025.

Spotify (4 February 2025b) 'Spotify Reports Fourth Quarter 2024 Earnings', *Spotify*. Available online:https://newsroom.spotify.com/2025-02-04/spotify-reports-fourth-quarter-2024-earnings/

Spoto, Alex (July 2012) 'Inside Tame Impala and Melody's Echo Chamber's Unlikely Partnership', *SPIN*. Available online: https://www.spin.com/2012/07/inside-tame-impala-and-melodys-echo-chambers-unlikely-partnership/

Stassen, Murray (December 2020) 'I Figured out a Really Long Time Ago That I Work for the Artist, They Don't Work for Me', *Music Business Worldwide*. Available online: https://www.musicbusinessworldwide.com/jodie-regan-tame-impala-i-figured-out-a-really-long-time-ago-that-i-work-for-the-artist-they-dont-work-for-me/

Stratton, Jon (2007) *Australian Rock. Essays on Popular Music*. Perth: API Network Books.

Stratton, Jon. 'The Triffids: The Sense of a Place', *Popular Music and Society*, vol. 30, no. 3, 2007, pp. 377–99.

Stratton, Jon (October 2008) 'The Difference of Perth Music: A Scene in Cultural and Historical Context', *Continuum: Journal of Media & Cultural Studies*, vol. 22, no. 5, pp. 613–22.

Stratton, Jon and Trainer, Adam (2016) 'Nothing Happens Here: Songs about Perth' in Jon Stratton and Peter Beilharz (Eds.) special issue of *Thesis Eleven on Western Australia*.

Stratton, Jon and Dale, Jon with Mitchell, Tony (2020) *An Anthology of Australian Albums*. New York: Bloomsbury Academic.

Tan, Steffanie (July 2018) 'Tame Impala Fans Worship Their Divine Lord Kevin Parker at Splendour', *Pedestrian.TV*. Available online: https://www.pedestrian.tv/music/fans-worship-kevin-parker/

Taylor, Gracie (2016) 'Kevin Parker: "Tame Impala Is Not a Band"'. Available online: https://www.nzherald.co.nz/entertainment/kevin-parker-tame-impala-is-not-a-band/R2GMCXE3KKPLLDC3FSOR6XKQIQ/

Telepathic Instruments (2024) *Telepathicinstruments.com*. Available online: https://telepathicinstruments.com/products/orchid-limited-pre-release

Terry, Josh (7 November 2019) 'Tame Impala Is the Artist of the Decade', *Vice*. Available online: https://www.vice.com/en/article/tame-impala-is-the-artist-of-the-decade/

Thompson, Daniel Jay (2025) *silverchair's Frogstomp*. New York: Bloomsbury Academic.

Tiny Mix, Tapes (12 July 2015) 'Tame Impala – Currents', tinymixtapes.com. Available online: https://www.tinymixtapes.com/music-review/tame-impala-currents

Trainer, Adam (2016) 'Perth Punk and the Construction of Urbanity in a Suburban City' *Popular Music*, vol. 35, no. 1, pp. 110–17.

triple j (1 July 2015) interview for recording song intros.

triple j (7 April 2016) 'Ali Barter Covers Tame Impala for Like A Version'. Available online: https://www.abc.net.au/triplej/programs/like-a-version-podcast/ali-barter-covers-tame-impala-for-like-a-version/11067654 triple j (July 2018) 'Tame Impala - The Less I Know The Better', *Inspired* hosted by Linda Marigliano. Available online: https://www.abc.net.au/triplej/programs/mornings/inspired-kevin-parker-tame-impala/9885370

triple j (14 March 2020) 'Kevin Parker Reacts to Tame Impala Winning Hottest 100 with "The Less I Know The Better"', triple j video'. Available online: https://www.abc.net.au/triplej/programs/triplej-breakfast/kevin-parker-reacts-to-tame-impala-the-less-i-know-the-better/12056944

triple j (November 2023) 'WATCH: Dua Lipa on Her Collab with Kevin Parker', *triple j*. Available online: https://www.abc.net.au/triplej/programs/drive/drive-dua-lipa-interview-video/103120250

Weber, Heike (2009) 'Taking Your Favorite Sounds Along: Portable Audio Technologies for Mobile Music Listening' in K. Bijsterveld and J. van Dijck (Eds.) *Sound Souvenirs: Audio Technologies, Memory, and Cultural Practices*. Amsterdam: Amsterdam University Press, pp. 69–82.

Weiner, Jonah (May 2019) 'The Cosmic Healing of Tame Impala', *Rolling Stone*. Available online: https://www.rollingstone.com/music/music-features/tame-impala-band-kevin-parker-836938/

Whish-Wilson, David (2013) *Perth*. Sydney: New South Publishers.

Who Is Daniel Johns? (November 2021) 'Daniel Talks to Kevin Parker', Spotify Studios. Available online: https://open.spotify.com/episode/2fJQntcSrtN8e7Lj4J0oFL

Wilkinson, Matt (26 February 2020) 'Tame Impala. Kevin Parker Picks the 5 Best Songs on Apple Music', *Apple Music*. Available online: https://music.apple.com/us/station/tame-impala/ra.1500454420

Wood, Mikael (25 August 2016) 'FYF Fest: Tame Impala's Kevin Parker Is Making Behind-the-Scenes Moves toward Pop', *LA Times*. Available online https://www.latimes.com/entertainment/music/la-et-ms-kevin-parker-fyf-20160822-snap-story.html

Zammitt, David (11 July 2015) 'Kevin Parker Sees His New Third Album as Tame Impala as a Fork in the Road', *Loud And Quiet*. Available online: https://www.loudandquiet.com/interview/kevin-parker-sees-new-third-album-tame-impala-fork-road/

Zentner, Alejandro (April 2006) 'Measuring the Effect of Online Piracy on Music Sales' *The Journal of Law & Economics*, vol. 49, no. 1, pp. 63–90.

Index

070 Shake 100
10cc 58
2Pac 30

ABC (Australian Broadcasting Commission) 20
AC/DC 34
Adele 111
Aerosmith 76
AFL (Australian Football League) 34
Air 8, 69
All Our Exes Live In Texas 100
Allbrook, Nick 10, 15–16, 25–31, 110
alternative rock 8, 10, 19–20, 26
Ammonia 21, 109
Apple Music 9, 93 *see also* Spotify, streaming service, Tidal, YouTube
APRA (Australasian Performing Rights Association) 4
Arctic Monkeys 91, 111
ARIA (Australian Recording Industry Association) 94, 97, 111–12
ARIA Awards 4, 104
artwork 49, 96, 109
A$AP Rocky 103
astronomy studies 11, 15–16, 109
Avalanches, The 16, 100
Avery, Cameron 10, 37, 110

Babe Rainbow, The 30
Baby Animals 19
Barbagallo, Julien 10
Barnett, Courtney 2
Barter, Ali 77, 100
bass 10, 42, 54–5, 57, 60–1, 64–6, 69, 71, 75, 78, 81–3, 85, 100, 103
Beach Boys, The 14
Beard, Wives, Denim 16
Beatles, The 7, 14, 25, 43, 111 *see also* Lennon, John
Beatty, Robert 49
Bee Gees 8, 51, 66, 76
Beethoven, Ludwig van 83
Berlin 27, 29
'Beverly Laurel' 37
Birds of Tokyo 21, 110
Blue Cheer 7
blues rock 15, 21
Bob Evans 32
Bon Iver 10
Bone Thugs-N-Harmony 62
Brainticket 25
break-off 63–4, 68, 80, 87 *see also* break-up, heartbreak
break-up 12, 32, 37, 59, 61, 63–4, 79, 81 *see also* break-off, heartbreak
Brisbane, Queensland 19
BRIT Awards 4
Byrne, David 94

call-and-response 55, 69–70 *see also* counter-melody
Caribou 52
Cars, The 58
'Cause I'm A Man' 63, 74–7, 82, 110
Cave, Nick 34
CD (scratched/skipping) 5, 46–7, 50, 66, 79
changes 9, 20, 44–5, 49, 54–6, 58–9, 64, 73, 79, 82, 84, 86, 99, 102, 108 *see also* transformation
Cheap Nasties, The 19
Chemical Brothers, The 43
Clapton, Eric 90, 111
collaboration/collaborator 10, 11–13, 23, 26, 38, 40, 63, 66, 89, 99–104
Collins, Phil 58
compact disc (CDs) 9, 97, 110
Confidence Man 100
counter-melody 4, 48, 70, 79, 83, 86 *see also* call-and-response
Cream 7, 25
Crowded House 100
Curtin University of Technology 15

'Daffodils' 38–9
Daft Punk 8, 43, 46, 48, 52, 100
dance music 2, 4, 8, 37, 43, 45, 60, 66, 95, 104
Death By Denim 30
Dee Dee Dums, The 15, 25
demo (recording) 16, 22, 24, 48, 58, 64, 102

Demon Fuzz 25
'Disciples' 53, 65, 71–4, 80, 85, 89–90
disco 2, 8, 38, 43, 51, 64–6, 68
Doors, The 25, 43, 111
Drake 111
Drapht 21
drugs 49–53
    blunt smoke 103
    pot 25
    stoner 2, 7, 31
    weed 25, 33, 51–2
drums 4, 8, 14, 41, 44, 49, 54–5, 57, 59–61, 65–6, 70–1, 79, 82, 102
    cymbal 50, 60, 82
Dungen 7
Dury, Ian 111
Dylan, Bob 58, 105

Electric Blue Acid Dogs 15
electronic music 3, 8, 37, 43, 46, 101, 107
'Elephant' 7, 53, 59, 77, 100
Empire of the Sun 21
End of Fashion 21, 24, 26
Epstein, Luke 15
Eskimo Joe 16, 21, 23, 26, 32, 109
'Eventually' 12, 59–63, 67, 69–71, 80–2, 100

Facebook 22, 91
fandom 50–1, 53, 73–4, 83, 107, 112
'Feels Like We Only Go Backwards' 7, 53, 103

finger-snaps 55, 57, 60, 66, 69, 75, 81, 84, 86
Flaming Lips, The 7, 59, 99
Fleetwood Mac 8, 97
Flume 2, 91
Foo Fighters 10
Fridmann, Dave 42
funk 2, 8, 25, 38–9, 66, 68, 75, 83

Gaye, Marvin 76
Goa 8, 44–5
Goetze, Glen 16, 109
Gorillaz 11, 99
'Gossip' 53, 62
Gotye 91
Grammy Awards 4, 92, 104
Great Gable 30
grunge rock 6, 8, 20, 30, 74
guitar(s) 5, 7, 13–14, 41, 43, 45–9, 54–5, 59, 62, 64–6, 71, 73, 75, 78–9, 81–2, 85–6, 111
Gum 90
Gyroscope 23–4

Haim 77
'Half Full Glass Of Wine' 21
heartbreak 59–60, 64, 67, 76 see also break-up, break-off
Hendrix, Jimi 15
Hilltop Hoods 111
hip hop 3, 37, 46–7, 69, 102–4 see also Rap
Hoodoo Gurus 19

indie (independent music) 8, 10, 95, 101

InnerSpeaker 1–3, 7, 29, 33, 38, 44, 47, 49, 64, 97, 112
Instagram 91, 112
internet fandom 12, 89–91
INXS 19
isolation 7, 17–19, 22–3, 26–9, 32, 75

Jackson, Michael 8, 38, 54, 74–5
Jagger, Mick 11, 100
Jebediah 21, 23, 26
Jefferson Airplane 25
Joel, Billy 30
John Butler Trio 21, 32, 109
John XXIII College 14
Johns, Daniel 5–6
Justice 11, 104

Kid Cudi 103
King Gizzard & The Lizard Wizard 30, 90

Lady Gaga 11, 102, 104
Lamar, Kendrick 11, 103, 112
Lawrence Parker, Sophie 63, 66, 68, 70–1, 79–80, 84, 91
Lazy Eyes, The 30
'Leaving Los Feliz' 39
Led Zeppelin 15
Lennon, John 1, 7 see also The Beatles
'Jealous Guy' 81
'Let It Happen' 1, 3–5, 37, 43–50, 53–5, 66, 69–71, 79–80, 83, 92, 100
Lipa, Dua 11, 102, 104
Little Birdy 21, 24, 109

lo-fi 2, 37, 72–3, 85
Lonerism 1–3, 7, 32–3, 35, 37, 44, 47, 49, 53, 56, 63–4, 74–5, 79, 97, 103–4, 112
Lopez, Jennifer 75
Lorde 91
Los Angeles 19, 30, 34
'Love/Paranoia' 80–2

Madonna 62
mainstream 9, 20, 26, 84, 94, 96, 99, 101–2
Martin, Max 102
Mathieson, Craig 20, 43
Maxo Cream 103
May, Abbe 35
Mayer, John 103, 112
Meg Mac 100
Melbourne, Victoria 17, 19, 26, 102
meme 10, 90–1
Methyl Ethel 110
Miguel 11, 99
Mini Mansions 100
Mink Mussel Creek 15–16, 25, 31, 99
Minogue, Kylie 34
Monkees, The 43, 111
motif 40, 49, 55, 60, 65–6, 70, 83–6
Motley Crüe 76
music festivals 3, 20, 45, 50, 89, 92, 97–8
    Big Day Out 20–1, 43
    Coachella 98, 103
    Future Music Festival 38
    Glastonbury 102
    Splendour In The Grass 91
MySpace 16, 22

'Nangs' 49–53, 62, 71
'New Person, Same Old Mistakes' 3, 73, 83–7, 99–101
New York 27, 30, 42
Newsom, Joanna 94
Ngaiire 100
Nine Inch Nails 10
Nirvana 97
Northlane 100

Ocean, Frank 59

P. Diddy 62
Panda Band 23
Panics, The 21
Paris 32, 35, 43, 46, 63, 81, 104
Parker, Jerry 13–15, 109
Parker, Rosalind 13
Parker, Steve 13
Parkin, Cam 38
'Past Life' 12, 63, 68–71, 73, 80
Perry, Katy 102, 105
Perth 11–36, 63, 91, 107, 110
    see also venues, Western Australia
Pink Floyd 1
podcast 5, 10, 98
Pond 16, 25–6, 90, 99
pop music 2–4, 7–8, 11, 20–1, 37–9, 46–7, 51, 53, 60, 64, 68, 71, 75, 84, 96, 99, 101–2, 107
'Powerlines' 12, 35
Presets, The 16
Prince 10, 74
Prochet, Melody 63, 71, 73, 79–80, 99

production 2, 7, 11–12, 14, 30, 39–42, 47, 50, 52–3, 61, 71–2, 99, 101–2, 104
progressive rock 2, 25, 43, 47
psychedelic music 2, 15, 25, 30, 43, 47, 51, 70, 74–5, 95
Psychedelic Porn Crumpets 30
psychedelic rock 1–2, 7–8, 26, 30–1, 51, 73, 91, 96, 100–1, 107 *see also* rock music
Public Enemy 30
publications
 Billboard 92, 100, 112
 Esquire 90
 GQ 93
 Grantland 97
 Guardian, The 29, 51
 Junkee 91
 NME 6, 8, 39, 73, 81, 92
 NZ Herald, The 10
 Observer, The 76
 Pedestrian.TV 91
 Pitchfork 42, 63, 84, 92
 Rolling Stone 4, 92
 Stereogum 92
 Under The Radar 48
 VICE 50, 98
punk music 5–6, 8, 19, 28, 31

Queen 97, 105

R&B 2, 8, 37, 47, 59, 62, 64, 68–9, 74–6, 99–100, 104
radio 20, 47, 72–3, 85 *see also* triple j
Radiohead 69
rap 11, 101–4, 107 *see also* hip hop
'Reality In Motion' 78–80
record labels
 Modular Recordings 10, 16, 22
 Sony Music Publishing 104
 Universal Music (Australia) 16
reddit 38, 89
r/tameimpala 89–90
Regan, Jodie 15–16, 26, 101
remix 40, 77, 100
RIAA (Recording Industry Association of America) 92
Richie, Lionel 74
Rihanna 100–1, 104, 112
rock music 7–8, 21, 25, 31, 34, 42, 46–7, 51, 53, 59–60, 71, 74, 76–7, 84–5, 93, 97, 102–3, 107 *see also* psychedelic rock
Roland GR-55 55, 64–5
Roland Juno-106 52, 75, 81
Roland JV-1080 53, 62, 75, 81
Ronson, Mark 37–9, 52, 65–6, 100–2
Ross, Diana 11, 99
Rowe, Zan 44, 54, 110
Rubin, Rick 10
Rundgren, Todd 7
Ryan, 'Shiny' Joe 15–16, 25, 28, 90

sample 46, 53, 62, 66, 81, 85, 100
San Cisco 110
Scientists, The 19
Scott, Travis 11, 103–4
Shadows, The 14

Sia 2, 34, 111
Silverchair 5–6
Simper, Dominic 10, 14
Sinatra, Frank 30
Sleepy Jackson, The 21, 24
Slow Rush, The 86, 104
soft rock 8, 47, 56–8
'Solitude Is Bliss' 7, 33
Something in the Water 22, 26
soul music 2, 51, 76, 99
Soundcloud 22, 75
South Africa 13
South Fremantle Power Station 35–7, 55
Space Lime Peacock 25
Spacey Jane 110
Spears, Britney 7, 102
Spotify 5, 8–9, 64, 89, 93–6, 98 *see also* streaming service, Apple Music, Tidal, YouTube
Springsteen, Bruce 105
Stems, The 19
streaming service 8–9, 93–8, 111 *see also* Spotify, Apple Music, Tidal, YouTube
Streets, The 11
suburbia 18–19, 24, 26–9, 32, 110
$uicideboy$ 103
'Summer Breaking' 39
Supertramp 7, 14
Swift, Taylor 94, 102
Sydney, New South Wales 16–17, 19–20, 26

synthesizer (synth) 1, 4, 8, 31, 37, 41, 43–7, 49–50, 52–5, 57, 59, 61–2, 65–6, 69–70, 72, 75, 78–9, 81–3, 85–6, 102
SZA 11, 112

'Taxi's Here' 110
Tears For Fears 54
Telepathic Instruments 104
television (TV) 20, 62, 72
'The Less I Know The Better' 63–8, 82, 85, 91–2, 100, 102, 110–11
'The Moment' 3, 53–6, 70–1
Thile, Chris 100
Thundercat 100
Tidal 9, 93 *see also* Apple Music, Spotify, streaming service, YouTube
TikTok 92
TLC 75
transformation 3–4, 33, 44–5, 51, 59, 63–4, 69, 72–4, 83, 85–7, 93, 99 *see also* changes
Trevor 67–8, 91, 111
Triffids, The 19, 21, 32, 109–10
triple j 1, 20–1, 44, 91 *see also* radio
  Hottest 100 21, 91–2, 100, 109–10
  Like A Version 77, 100
Troy Terrace 15, 24–5, 28
Twitter (tweeted) 22, 90
Tyler, The Creator 103

Uchis, Kali 11, 99

Vance Joy 111
venues
    Fly By Night 25
    Mojos Bar 15, 25
    Newport Hotel, The 25
    Norfolk Basement, The 15, 25
    Railway Hotel, The 25
    Swan Basement, The 25
    see also Perth, Western Australia
Victims, The 19
vinyl 9, 14, 62, 64, 89, 97–9, 110
Violent Soho 91
vocal harmonies 60–1, 65, 69, 78, 81, 83
Vonnegut, Kurt 28

Waifs, The 21, 32
Warner, Dave (From The Suburbs) 19, 32
Watson, Jay 10, 15–16, 25, 28, 31, 38, 91
Weeknd, The 11, 99, 102
West, Kanye 11, 91, 103
Western Australia
    Albany 21
    Bunbury 33
    Busselton 33
    Coogee Beach 35
    Cottesloe 13
    Daglish 24, 28
    Fremantle 5, 15, 25, 34–6
    Injidup Beach 33
    Kalgoorlie 13
    Mandurah 18, 33, 109
    Margaret River 33
    Mt. Lawley 13
    Mount Claremont 14
    Subiaco 24–5
    Two Rocks 18
    see also Perth, venues
Wiggles, The 11, 100
Witt, Ben 37
Wolfmother 15–16
Wonder, Stevie 8, 10, 76

'Yes I'm Changing' 3, 12, 56–60, 63, 67, 70, 73, 80, 100
Yorke, Thom 94
YouTube 9, 22, 52, 67, 93 *see also* Apple Music, Spotify, streaming service, Tidal